Untying the Mystery—the Day of the Lord

Shane Carter

ISBN 978-1-0980-8379-3 (paperback)
ISBN 978-1-0980-8380-9 (digital)

Christian Faith Publishing, Inc.
832 Park Avenue
Meadville, PA 16335
www.christianfaithpublishing.com

Printed in the United States of America

Light, Life, and the Alpha Day

We must lay some foundational work before we can understand the Alpha (first) day of the Lord. Before Adam was in the garden and before the foundation of the world, God existed outside of this lower realm of time in the higher heaven. God's word from our perspective speaks of three heavens created.

The *first* heaven is the expanse around the earth where the birds fly. This expanse is our atmosphere, a part of this planet. We can be in the earth and on the earth at the same time. The *second* heaven is where the stars and planets abide. This expanse is enormous and mind-boggling to us, designed by our Creator to show us just how vast and glorious he is. Amen. The *third* heaven (2 Cor. 12:2) is the manifested dwelling place of Almighty God. The third heaven, for general understanding, is a bright, perfect, celestial body in an eternal expanse. Earth is a terrestrial body in an expanse that, although vast, has a boundary. It is a shadow copy of heaven. A shadow is a darker copy of an illuminated object but not the very object itself. The *third heaven* is in a higher dimension of light. This is why God said, "The heaven is my throne, and the earth is my footstool (Isa. 66:1). Please understand, the choices made on this shadowy planet are evidences of our main choice, and that choice is binding and eternal. What is the main choice? Light or darkness.

King David recognized this in the spirit and prayed:

> For we are strangers before thee, and *sojourners*, as were all our fathers: *our days on the earth are as a shadow*, and there is none abiding. (1 Chron. 29:15; emphasis mine).

Also in other books of the Bible:

> *For we are but of yesterday, and know nothing,* because our days upon earth are a shadow. (Job 8:9)

> *For who knoweth what is good for man in this life, all the days of his vain life* which he spendeth as a shadow? *for who can tell a man what shall be after him under the sun?* (Eccl. 6:12)

New Testament

> *Let no man therefore judge you in meat, or in drink, or in respect of an holyday, or of the new moon, or of the sabbath days: Which are a* shadow *of things to come; but the body is of Christ.* (Col. 2:16–17)

> *Who serve unto the example and* shadow of heavenly things, *as Moses was admonished of God when he was about to make the tabernacle: for, See, saith he, that thou make all things according to the pattern showed to thee in the mount.* (Heb. 8:5)

Why so much talk of shadows in the word? Well, it is because we are living on or in those shadows. Earth is a planet infected with death and is constantly turning with a shadow of darkness. This world is temporal, a shadow of the real life, which is in Christ Jesus.

He is heaven's life and light. With the creation of the solar system, the sun's light casts a shadow on the earth.

The *third heaven*, on the other hand, is the place where there are no shadows and where God created sons (angels) and different beings like seraphim (fiery creatures) and cherubim (living creatures). Heaven is a place of pure light where perfection dwells. There are no days there because there is no end to the light of God.

> *Every good gift and every perfect gift is from above, and cometh down from the Father of lights,* with whom is no variableness, neither *shadow* of turning. (Jas. 1:17)

One of the beings God created was Lucifer. Lucifer was a cherub whose job was to cover and carry the glory of God. Lucifer's name means "light bearer." However, Lucifer fell from his lofty position, corrupted by his own beauty. Most of the information about his origins and fall are written in Isaiah 14 (Lucifer the light bearer.) and Ezekiel 28 (king of Tyrus).

Lucifer decided that he would exalt himself to the status of being like the Most High. He thought that his beauty and communication skills (trafficking in his trade.) would be all he needed to accomplish this task. So how did Lucifer become the king of Tyrus? When God created Adam and Eve, he gave them dominion over all the earth. Lucifer knew this and made a plan to usurp this dominion. If he could get Adam and Eve to obey him (by yielding to his temptation), he would overcome them as slaves and have some security because he knew God loved his creation. Kings have kingdoms and kingdoms have dominion.

> *Know ye not, that to whom ye yield yourselves servants to obey, his servants ye are to whom ye obey;* whether of sin unto death, *or* of obedience unto righteousness. (Rom. 6:16)

If God was going to destroy Lucifer, God would also have to destroy Adam and Eve because they would be under Lucifer's dominion and, therefore, part of his estate or house. The two reasons he deceived them in the garden was to gain preservation and dominion. God, in his wisdom, saw Lucifer's plan and strangely (to us) granted his request not to be god of heaven, but of earth. This brilliant decision would, once and for all, answer the questions for both the children of light and the children of darkness: Who is worthy to be God? What would it be like if someone else were in charge? In addition, is God really just in his judgments?

Earth is a perfect place for these revelations. It is part light and part dark. You can taste of both good and evil and make your choice. It will reveal the intent of your heart, to you, and give all the experiences needed to make the choice. If you want to deny God and do your own thing as Satan, it will give you an excuse to choose not to believe God because you cannot see him. If you want to believe, it will reveal if you are just giving lip service or if your trust is real from the heart. Remember this is not a game, it is the manifestation of our hearts. Darkness goes to darkness and light to light!

This accomplishes many things. Once we are done on earth, we will not have to be acclimated to heaven because we will already be familiar with it. Of course, heaven is far more glorious than this dark copy called earth. We will not be subject to death, pain, sorrow, regret, sickness, and fleshly desires. "Thy kingdom come, Thy will be done on earth, as it is in heaven" as noted in the Lord's Prayer (Matt. 6:10). It is not just a concept. Heaven and earth will become one for all eternity with no more shadows.

Lucifer had enough self-awareness to think, *I am more beautiful than any other creature and more cunning than all my fellows, I should be worshipped.* I do not know how long he pondered this, but he did not cast the thought down. It took root in his heart and consumed him! The problem with Lucifer is that he sinned without a tempter, which is sin in the spirit. God made him perfect, but he transgressed willfully even though he knew the truth, which gave birth to a lie. There is no redemption for the transgression in the spirit.

*For if we sin wilfully after that we have received
the knowledge of the truth, there remaineth no more
sacrifice for sins.* (Heb. 10:26)

This proud presumption caused him to lose his God-given place, separating him from his Creator. Thus, evil was born. Evil is the lack of good. God is the very fabric of good. This painful sowing of selfish or self-willed behavior brought a harvest, which was the basis of his fall from heaven (Lk. 10:18). Lucifer was able to draw a third of the heavenly host, the "stars of heaven" (a metaphor for angels), into following him on his corrupted path (Rev. 12:4). Thus, the darkness (lack of light) consumed him. Like a falling star, he continues on his self-consuming path. Ironically, the bearer of light has now become the darkness. Once Lucifer changed his position, there was a need for a new title so he became known as Satan. Once Lucifer became Satan and his destiny changed, he took on an offensive position as "the accuser."

God knew this was going to happen. He did not stop it, choosing instead to create Lucifer with freewill. God is love, and love does not seek its own way (1 Cor. 13:5). If you are not allowed to choose the wrong thing, you never had a choice at all. Choosing the wrong thing has consequences. The consequences in this case are beyond our ability to imagine. It is separation from God, which means we have none of his goodness and none of his benefits. God is life so this separation is death. Death is a place, not merely a state of being or a termination from existence. It is a land of total separation from life. Death contains hell, and hell is completely free from anything good. It is freedom from God and what a horrific tormenting place.

This is why Jesus came to rescue us from Satan's corruption. Man can have redemption because he has the ability to have faith. Jesus came in the flesh to destroy sin in the flesh and make atonement for our souls (Rom. 8:3). The soul came about because God breathed life into the flesh (Gen. 2:7).

*Remember the former things of old: for I am God,
and there is* none *else; I am God, and there is* none

*like me, Declaring the end from the beginning, and
from ancient times the things that are not yet done,
saying,* My counsel shall stand, *and I will do all
my pleasure. (Isa. 46:9–10, emphasis added)*

God knew when he made the earth and placed Adam on it that
Adam was going to fall to Satan. In the same way, he knew Lucifer
was going to fall. So does this mean he created them purposefully
to fall? No, it just means that he allowed them to choose and, based
on their choices, made a plan of redemption and punishment. If
God did not allow them to fall, then they had no choice. The Lord
God chose not to invest in a spirit or way of life that is not good. Of
course, as soon as someone falls, the blame game starts. Punishment
is not what God wants, but if you chose to reject him, it is all that
is left!

God put the tree of knowledge of good and evil in the garden
not so much as a test of man's faithfulness, but for the manifestation
of the truth, best said by his own words.

*I am the vine, ye are the branches: He that abideth
in me, and I in him, the same bringeth forth much
fruit: for* without me ye can do nothing. (John
15:5)

Adam & Eve sinned because they acted independently and did
not abide in God's word. It is *impossible* for anyone to do good or
function with a pure motive without being connected to the source
of good (God). This is the wisdom of this life and its lesson. The only
people who think it is possible to live without God are the children
of *pride*. God, knowing that man could not connect to an all-power-
ful holy God without a connecting port, made a decision that one of
Godhead would have to become a man, representing both. This job
fell to God's Son, Jesus Christ. This was determined before creation.

*That it might be fulfilled which was spoken by the
prophet, saying, I will open my mouth in parables;*

> *I will utter things which have been kept secret* from the foundation of the world. (Matt. 13:35)

> *And all that dwell upon the earth shall worship him, whose names are not written in the book of life of the Lamb slain* from the foundation of the world. (Rev. 13:8)

God did not create anything without making it through Jesus (His Word). When God starts a project, he looks all the way through the process and finishes it before he begins. That way, it will be perfect. There is no surprises for him!

Now that this understanding is in place, let's look at the creation process to understand the Alpha Day. (The bold type will be our subject text.)

> *In the beginning God created the heaven and the earth. The earth was without form, and void; and darkness was on the face of the deep. And the Spirit of God moved upon the face of the waters. And God said,* **Let there be light: and there was light.** (Gen. 1:1–3; emphasis added).

When God spoke "Let there be light," Jesus came into the physical via a spiritual avenue (John 8:12). Our eyes were created to receive light because they are the windows to our souls, which is the place our hearts reside. When this light came out of the darkness, it did so in this physical realm as the face of Jesus. He is the glory of God.

> *For God, who commanded the light to shine out of darkness, hath shined in our hearts, to give the light of the knowledge of the* glory *of God in the face of* Jesus Christ. (2 Cor. 4:6)

This then is the message which we have heard of him, and declare unto you, that God is light, and in him is no darkness at all. (1 John 1:5)

Jesus, whose name means "Jehovah (God) is salvation," is the Light and sustainer of all life. Light is salvation because it takes light to produce and sustain life. God manifested his Son, which is the love of his life, when he spoke the words "be Light"—or, for a deeper understanding, "be Me." Then came the birth of light in creation, which is the manifestation of the glory of God to the earth. When God spoke his word, he was speaking through Jesus because *Jesus is the Word*. This is noted in the books of Psalms and Revelation.

Thy word *is a lamp unto my feet, and a* light *unto my path.* (Ps. 119:105)

And he was clothed with a vesture dipped in blood: and his name is called The Word of God. (Rev. 19:13)

This is the first recorded word that God spoke, and that Light was the Word.

In the beginning was the Word, *and the* Word *was with God, and the Word was God. The same was in the beginning with God. All things were made by him; and without him was not anything made that was made. In him was life; and the life was the light of men. And the light shineth in darkness; and the darkness comprehended it not.* (John 1:1–5)

Let this sink in deep, if God manifests himself in *word* or *light*, it is *always* Jesus! Genesis 1:4 notes, "And God saw the light, that it was good: and God divided the light from the darkness." After God manifested, he moved into the sanctification process. In God, there is no darkness. In fact, in him is the only place you can be free from darkness. Therefore, *God has divided (separated) the Light and the darkness* and is continuing to do so. This brings about holiness (set apart). Darkness, on the other hand, is a lack of light and understanding, which is a lack of God. Genesis 1:5 reads, "And God called the light Day, and the darkness he called Night. And the evening and the morning were the *first day*."

God called the light "day" because the birth of Light ushered in the birth of time. God knew that light in the physical travels and is measurable; therefore, he named the measurement *day*, which is the time the light is present. A day can *only* exist inside of time because it has a beginning and an ending. For example, there are, on average, twelve hours of light in a day here on earth (John 11:9). In heaven, there is no measurement of time. It is eternal, therefore a "day" does not exist. The light has no beginning and no ending because there is no time. There is no shadow of turning as it happens upon the earth. The word for day here in Hebrew is *yom*, meaning "to be hot." It represents the time the light is present for twelve hours or so—longer or shorter, depending on your location and perspective. Light, with its speed and illumination, allows us to understand science and is the foundation of time in this realm. Science was given by God so that we could understand and pursue his goodness.

This birth of light is the first day of this creation (Rev. 1:8). Jesus is the firstborn of all, which was this first Light. I believe this is why the Bible records, *"I will declare the decree: the Lord hath said unto me, Thou art my Son; this day have I begotten thee"* (Ps. 2:7).

In order to be part of time, you must be born in it. Jesus must be first of all things because he is God's representative. Since God is the source of all things, it is right for him to have first place. This is why Paul, through the Holy Spirt, wrote:

> *For by him were all things created, that are in*
> *heaven, and that are in earth, visible and invisible,*
> *whether they be thrones, or dominions, or principal-*
> *ities, or powers: all things were created by him, and*
> *for him: And he is before all things, and by him all*

*things consist. And he is the head of the body, the
church: who is the beginning, the firstborn from the
dead; that in* all *things he might have the* preemi-
nence. (Col. 1:16–18)

That which is flesh is flesh; that which is spirit is spirit (John
3:6). Jesus, the manifested Light, revealed his true spiritual identity by shining in this physical world during creation. Jesus and the
Father are one. Jesus would later be born into flesh to manifest himself as a man. These two manifestations point to the truth of who
he is. The reason he is named the Son of God is that he also became
man. Those who choose to receive his Light can be born again and
will not have to live in darkness, spiritual or physical, and be called
the sons of God!

*Light is sown for the righteous, and gladness for the
upright in heart.* (Ps. 97:11)

*Who being the brightness of his glory [God's Light],
and the express image of his person [God's son], and
upholding all things by the word of his power [God's
Word], when he had by himself purged our sins,
sat down at the right hand of the Majesty on high.*
(Heb. 1:3; emphasis added)

Jesus, the "I am," was birthed as light, then as Abraham's seed,
and then from the dead as the resurrected Savior. This all happened
because he wants us to be connected to God.

*I in them, and thou in me, that they may be made
perfect in one; and that the world may know thou
hast sent me, and hast loved them, as thou hast loved
me.* (John 17:23)

Light brings revelation! If we walk into a dark room, we do not
have understanding as to what is present until the light is present.

The light gives us the understanding and keeps us from stumbling over things that the darkness is hiding. This is physical as well as spiritual. Light contains all the visible and invisible colors that exist. When we see an object, the color it appears to have is simply the color that is reflected in the light. This destroys all argument of a racial superiority because the color is in the light. Each gift God has given is in his body as it seemed good to him. This is why Joseph, a foreshadowing of Jesus the Christ, wore a coat of many colors.

> *Now Israel loved Joseph more than all his children, because he was the son of his old age: and he made him a coat of many colors.* (Gen. 37:3)

This coat symbolized that Jesus revealed himself as light and the colors reflect the nations. All those in Christ will become the children of light. Remember that this coat, dipped in the blood of a sacrificial animal, was done so to reveal that one must washed in the blood of Jesus.

It is important to note that in Genesis 1:16, God created the sun to light the earth physically in Jesus's physical absence. The sun's light is not the true light. However, it is a sign and a constant reminder of his salvation set in place until Jesus shines physically again on this earth. God, working in the same manner with both the earth and Jesus, took some clay and gave them the ability to sustain life within three days (the pattern of the resurrection). The sun, moon, and stars, created on the fourth day, were set up to give light in the absence of the physical manifestation of God's expressed image. All power in heaven and earth is radiating from his light.

Now that we know who the Light is (Jesus) and what a day is, we can understand the concept of the "Day of the Lord." The *Day of the Lord* is the light that is radiating from the being of God. God's manifestation is Jesus. Wherever his light shines in the heavenly or earthly realm, the Lord is present. The Lord must be the source of the light before the day can be of the Lord. The Light of the Lord is unlike the sunlight we experience on a daily basis. The Lord's Light is completely pure, penetrating to the very core of our being and illuminating everything contained therein. The Lord's Light and his Word are synonymous. What he sees or imagines, he speaks; what he speaks, he will see. His light is a pure, incorruptible light that will expose and consume corruption. For our sakes, God does not completely reveal himself until our completion because his light would consume everything not pure, holy, and eternal.

Let's sum up this chapter. The Day of the Lord is the Light that is coming from the Lord's being. That Light is Jesus. He was the first light to shine in creation. He is upholding everything; therefore, he is the Alpha (first) day; the expressed image of God. This first light was not the sun, it was the Son of God!

The Omega Day

I am the Alpha and Omega, the beginning and the ending, *says the Lord.*

—Revelation 1:8

In the prior chapter, we determined that the source of the first light was God's expressed image and that he is the Day (light) of the Lord. His light first revealed as the Alpha, the beginning of creation. So the question of this chapter is, what is the Omega (last) day of the Lord? To answer this question, a foundational issue must be addressed. God's word is a narrative story, a story about the revelation of his Son, and we are characters in the story.

For all our days are passed away in thy wrath: we spend our years as a tale that is told. (Ps. 90:9)

All of the truths given to complete his life's revelation are located in the volume of the book (Heb. 10:7). God has hidden the revelation. It is our duty to search out the matter (Prov. 25:2). As we chew on God's word, all the flavors of revelation are released as revealed by the Holy Spirit, which conveys the mind of Christ (John 16:15). If we look for interpretation outside of God's word, we *can be led anywhere*. Jesus is the beginning, and he will be the ending.

Let's look at what his word says about the Omega (last) day and its length of time. This information best understood from this verse:

> *But beloved be not* ignorant *of this one thing, that*
> one day *is with the Lord as a thousand years, and a*
> *thousand years as* one day. (2 Pet. 3:8)

First, this is the only verse in which the Holy Spirit commands us not to be ignorant of its content. It is like taking a quiz when you were in school. The teacher reviews the test material and he or she says with that certain look, "Pay attention to this because it is on the test and it is very important."

For the person who would say "God's not being literal. He is not talking about a thousand years. He's just talking about a long period of time," I would ask, why would God command us not to be ignorant or unaware of an obscure or undetermined amount of time? How can that be required? Furthermore, why would God then take the time to tell us forward and backward (two witness) that a day with the Lord is as a thousand years and a thousand years is as a day if it is just some mysterious frame of time? How could he phrase it any better than to say, "Be not ignorant"? Note this is *very* important to understand in order to discern the Day of the Lord. Being ignorant of this truth will blind you to all kinds of revelation in God's word, hence the command, "*be not ignorant.*"

Let's look at this verse closely. Second Peter 3:8 reads, "But, beloved, be not *ignorant* (to be unaware) that *one day* is (as opposed to a week or month of days) *with the Lord* (Jesus) *as* (adverb meaning like unto or equal with) a *thousand years* (a specific amount of time), and a thousand years as a *day* (the time light is present). In other words, the Day of the Lord is as a thousand years of earth time without shadow. This amount of time is part of God's overall plan for this creation. It is part of his perspective for the pattern of this earth age. Let's not be ignorant!

God's word always has at least two witnesses. With regard to this, earth time here is the second witness.

> *For a* thousand years *in* thy sight *are but as* yesterday *when it is past, and as a watch in the night.* (Ps. 90:4)

From God's prospective, a thousand years on earth is one divine day. Please remember that from God's prospective, the sun is continually shining on earth. Earth is simply rotating to create day and night. Therefore, our perspective is not his perspective. "As a watch in the night" is referring to the fact that on this planet when a thousand years passes under the sun, it so pales to the brightness of his light. It is like the darkness of nighttime. How important is this truth? This brings revelation to the word of God pertaining to Adam's transgression.

> *But of the tree of the knowledge of good and evil thou shalt not eat of it for* in the day *that thou eat thereof thou shalt surely die.* (Gen. 2:17)

> *And all the days that Adam lived were* nine hundred and thirty years: *and he died.* (Gen. 5:5)

A day with the Lord is as a thousand years. Adam died at 930, so he died within the divine day from God's prospective. There is no mystery here, only a misunderstanding of God's heavenly perspective. In other words, the death sentence must take place in less than one thousand years. No one in the flesh that has the curse in their blood can live a thousand years.

One of the best places in scripture to find information on this Omega day is Revelation chapter 20. First, understand that when Jesus returns, he will reign for a thousand years, the same amount of time that books of 2 Peter and the Psalms record is equal to a day with the Lord. It is not an ambiguous time, it is exactly a thousand years. This is most widely known as the millennial reign, which comes from the word *millennium*, meaning a thousand years.

This is where the light turns on, pardon the pun. The New Testament's millennial reign is the Old Testament's Day of the Lord— or as Paul puts it, the Day of Christ—mentioned in 1 Corinthians 1:8, Philippians 1:6–10, Philippians 2:16, etc. In simple words, Jesus will be here shining for a thousand years, which is *one* of his days.

In the Old Testament Jesus's name was not known so the prophets referred to his reigning period as the Day of the Lord. Now we have the New Testament and we know that Jesus Christ is the Light, we have a better understanding. Also consider this, this is the last day that light will shine on this earth, chasing away its shadow. This day will be worldwide and a thousand years in length. Jesus stated:

> *Heaven and earth shall pass away, but my words shall not pass away.* (Matt. 24:35)

This last day is the Sabbath day of this creation, the seventh, one-thousand-year, period in this creation: the time of his rest. This is the reason Jesus healed so many people on the Sabbath day; to show that he is the rest. He is the Sabbath, in him is the fulfilling of the Sabbath day. (Hebrews 4:3-9) It is also the reason Jesus made the comment

> *For the Son of Man is* Lord *even of the* sabbath day. (Matt. 12:8)

Every word that Jesus speaks has a prophetic meaning and must happen at some time. For as the scripture says, the testimony of Jesus is the spirit of prophecy (Rev. 19:10). We can see the Day of the Lord as we follow this chapter until verse 4. Keep in mind these passages are from Revelation 20:1–4. (Again bold type is our anchor scriptures.)

1. ***And I saw an angel come down from heaven, having the key of the bottomless pit and a great chain in his hand.***
   An angel is dispatched to complete the binding of Satan (darkness), and he is using a great chain to accom-

plish his objective. Sin creates bondage. How fitting it is to bind the father of lies.

2. *And he laid hold on the dragon, that old serpent, which is the Devil, and Satan, and bound him* **a thousand years.**

   Satan will be bound for a thousand years during the Day of the Lord. He will be unable to tempt or deceive anyone with his darkness. In the Light, rest will come. Jesus is fulfilling his prophecy of being the light of the world, and his light is shining because there is no darkness at all. This means physically and spiritually during this last day, *his day*.

3. *And cast him into the bottomless pit, and shut him up, and set a seal upon him, that he should deceive the nations no more, till the thousand years should be fulfilled: and after that he must be loosed a little season.*

   After being chained in the bottomless pit for a thousand years, Satan will tempt those who were born during those years on the earth once released. This darkness from Satan will cause the day of the Lord to end and eternity revealed.

4. *And I saw thrones, and they sat upon them, and judgment was given unto them: and I saw the souls of them that were beheaded for the witness of Jesus, and for the word of God, and which had not worshipped the beast, neither his image, neither had received his mark upon their foreheads, or in their hands; and they lived and reigned with Christ a thousand years.*

   The thrones that John saw will include the twelve disciples (Matt. 19:28). The beast (Antichrist) wreaking havoc on the earth during the tribulation period by destroying God's saints will finally end. By this, we know that the Day of the Lord starts after the tribulation period, not during it.

I would like to offer more evidence of this truth. The key event that the Day of the Lord is about to start is the end of the age, which is the end of the sun's existence in the *solar system*. What changes the age is the fact that the sun is no longer the light of this world. As indicated in chapter 1, the sun is a representation of the Son of God until he returns physically to be the Light of the Word (John 8:12). During the Day of the Lord, there is no need for the sun because the Lord's light is comparable to the sun but brighter (Matt. 17:2, Acts 26:13, and Rev. 1:16).

The two verses that place the time of the Day of the Lord in relationship to the sun darkening are Matthew 24:29 and Joel 2:31.

> *Immediately after the tribulation of those days shall the* sun be darkened, *and the moon shall not give her light, and the stars shall fall from heaven, and* the powers of the heavens shall be shaken. (Matt. 24:29)

After the tribulation period, the sun will go dark. This is no cloud going over it or a solar eclipse. It will just be extinguished! This is evident by the "stars shall fall from heaven and the powers of the heavens being shaken." When the powers of the second heaven are shaken, that is the *breakup* of the solar system, resulting in the sun darkening and the earth losing its orbit.

> *Therefore I will shake the heavens,* and the earth shall remove out of her place, *in the wrath of the Lord of hosts, and* in the day of his fierce anger. (Isa. 13:13)

Earth's place in the heavens is in orbit around the sun. This shaking will take place to mark the new age that will no longer be under the sun.

> *What [is] that which hath been? It [is] that which is, and what [is] that which hath been done? It [is]*

> *that which is done, and* there is not an entirely
> new thing under the sun. (Eccl. 1:9 YLT)

The sun cannot be present when this new thing (the Day of the Lord) takes place.

> The sun shall be turned into darkness, *and the*
> *moon into blood,* before *the great and the terrible*
> *day of the Lord come.* (Joel 2:31)

We can see by these verses that after the tribulation and before the Day of the Lord, the sun loses its place and power. The Day of the Lord begins after the tribulation period, so says Jesus:

> *Immediately after the tribulation of those days shall*
> *the* sun be darkened, *and the moon shall not give*
> *her light, and the stars shall fall from heaven, and*
> the powers of the heavens shall be shaken: And
> then *shall appear the sign of the Son of man in*
> *heaven: and then shall all the tribes of the earth*
> *mourn, and they shall see the Son of man coming*
> *in the clouds of heaven with power and great glory.*
> (Matt. 24:29–30)

This is supported throughout the Old Testament. With each piece of the puzzle in place, a picture starts to form. Here are some of the sources:

> *Which commanded* the sun, *and it rises not; and*
> *sealeth up the stars.* (Job 9:7)

> *For the stars of heaven and the constellations thereof*
> *shall not give their light:* the sun shall be darkened
> in his going forth, *and the moon shall not cause her*
> *light to shine.* (Isa. 13:10)

Then the moon shall be confounded, and the sun ashamed, *when the Lord of hosts shall reign in mount Zion, and in Jerusalem, and before his ancients gloriously.* (Isa. 24:23)

The sun shall be no more thy light by day; *neither for brightness shall the moon give light unto thee: but the Lord shall be unto thee an everlasting light, and thy God thy glory.* Thy sun shall no more go down; *neither shall thy moon withdraw itself: for the Lord shall be thine everlasting light, and the days of thy mourning shall be ended.* (Isa. 60:19–20)

The sun and the moon shall be darkened, *and the stars shall withdraw their shining.* (Joel 3:15)

In the light of Jesus Christ, old things become new.

And he that sat upon the throne said, Behold, I make all things new. *And he said unto me, Write: for these words are true and faithful.* (Rev. 21:5)

In order for the Day of the Lord to be on the earth, the presence of the Lord has to be revealed. That means physically, as Zephaniah proclaims:

Hold thy peace at the presence of the Lord God: for the day of the Lord is at hand: *for the Lord hath prepared a sacrifice, he hath bid his guests.* (Zeph. 1:7)

To further understand that the sun will no more be the light of this world, consider this statement:

They shall hunger no more, neither thirst anymore; neither shall the sun light on them, *nor any heat.* (Rev. 7:16).

In this passage, the redeemed are promised that the sun will no longer light or shine on them because it is no longer the light of this earth.

Now that we know the Lord takes the place of the sun, let's look at the process in which this takes place. It is outlined in Zechariah 14 (Bold type will be out anchor scriptures).

1. ***Behold, the day of the Lord is coming, and your spoil will be divided in your midst.*** (KJV)

2. ***For I will gather all nations against Jerusalem to battle; and the city shall be taken, and the houses rifled, and the women ravished; and half of the city shall go forth into captivity, and the residue of the people shall not be cut off from the city.***

   This section opened with two verses. One speaks of a notification that this glorious day is approaching, and the second is a warning of the tribulation that precedes it.

3. ***Then the Lord will go forth and fight against those nations, As He fights in the day of battle.***

   This verse is speaking of the battle of Armageddon, which will take place as his kingdom of light begins shining into the darkness, thus being introduced into this realm and creating a new age no longer under the light of the sun.

4. ***And in** that **day His feet will stand on the Mount of Olives, which faces Jerusalem on the east. And the Mount of Olives shall be split in two, from east to west,** Making a very large valley; Half of the mountain shall move toward the north and half of it toward the south.*

   Jesus's feet will return from where they left at the ascension (Acts 1:6–9). The angel said he would return in like manner. The Mount of Olives is where olives are grown. Olive oil was used to fuel the lamps of the temple and for anointing. The old way of lighting the temple will not be needed because the anointed one who is the true light will dwell with us.

5. ***Then you shall flee* through *My mountain valley, For the mountain valley shall reach to Azal. Yes, you shall flee as you fled from the earthquake in the days of Uzziah king of Judah. Thus the Lord my God will come,* and *all the saints with You*.**

There will be a passageway for the 144,000 and the remnant of Israel to return to Zion (Revelation 14) at that time, and Jesus will return with all that are in him.

6. ***It shall come to pass in that day* that *there will be no light; the lights will diminish*.**

Jesus will return like a thief in the night. This is evident by the solar system and heavenly luminaries being extinguished and dissolved (2 Pet. 3:10). The Day of the Lord will start as any day starts in darkness until the day has fully dawned. The sun, moon, and stars were set forth as signs, and the signs are telling the story of the fall and redemption process of men. The Day of the Lord is the fulfillment of the story.

7. ***It shall be *one* day Which is known to the Lord-Neither day nor night. But at evening time it shall happen *That* it will be light*.**

Jesus, the Light, will reign for one day (the Lord's divine day of one thousand years), which will be an intimate time with our bridegroom King. This day will be a thousand-year day that is continually without darkness. Heaven on earth. This will happen because it will not be day or night under the current sun, which causes day and night. In him, there is no shadow of turning. Instead of darkness ending the day, the light of the Lord will continue to shine throughout the day. This will last uninterrupted for a thousand years. There will be no darkness, physically or spiritually, because both heaven and earth will be one. The day will end after the thousand years as Satan is released, bringing his darkness to tempt those who were born in that day. Unfortunately, the ruler of darkness will return once again to end this last great day.

8. *And in that day it shall be* **that** *living waters shall flow from Jerusalem, Half of them toward the eastern sea And half of them toward the western sea; In both summer and winter it shall occur.*

    The Holy Spirit (river of life) will flow through the land physically because the spiritual world will be one with this physical world. The real will merge with is shadow copy. It is bringing to pass the Lord's Prayer, especially "thy kingdom come thy will be done on earth as it is in heaven."

9. *And the Lord shall be King over all the earth.* **In that day** *it shall be— "'The Lord is one,'" And His name one.*

    Jesus is the King of kings and Lord of lords! There will be kings and lords over different areas of the earth as Elohim wills. God is one (Father, Son, and Holy Spirit), and we will be one with them. We shall rule as one. More evidence of this truth is revealed in the transfiguration account located in the gospels.

Let's look at Matthews account:

1. *And after six days Jesus taketh Peter, James, and John his brother, and bringeth them up into an high mountain apart*
2. *And was transfigured before them: and* his face did shine as the sun, *and his raiment was white as the light. (Matthew 7)*

This vision is pointing to the fact that this is the seventh day, which is the Day of the Lord or the Sabbath (rest) of creation. Jesus takes Peter, James, and John and goes to a high mountain where he is transfigured. This is how he will appear in the Day of the Lord. He will become the sun and be the light of the world just as the Old Testament prophets saw him in their visions of old. In addition, just like the first (Alpha) day of creation, his face will once again enlighten the earth.

Let's sum up this chapter. Jesus is the Light in the Day of the Lord, and that day is the millennial rein. The day will dawn with his revelation from heaven. He will be the Light of the world for a thousand years. Satan will be bound during this time and will be loosed for a season to end the day after the thousand years are fulfilled. This is the last day of this creation, the Omega day!

Resurrection

As we begin this controversial subject, keep in mind we are on a pursuit of the truth. No matter which way you view this subject, it will come to pass as God's word declares. Simply believing a doctrine deeply is not enough. God's word must bear witness. Truth is not determined by emotion, fear of the unknown, or desire of the human heart. The truth is, Jesus is the Word of God. In his light, there is revelation. All scripture must agree together without exception.

Jesus proclaims that he is the resurrection, *"Jesus said unto her, I am the resurrection, and the life: he that believeth in me, though he were dead, yet shall he live"* (John 11:25). The depth of this statement points to the truth that God is the source of life (John 1:4). In order for the resurrection to happen, the Light of Jesus, which is the life of men, must be manifested. When Jesus died on the cross, darkness was upon his face. This is evident by the sign that represents him, which is the sun becoming dark, as the Father laid our sins to his charge on Calvary (Matt. 27:45). He laid in darkness three days before his light once again shown as it did in the beginning.

Let's look at one of the most well-known passages about the future resurrection in the Bible. (Bold type is our anchor scriptures.)

For the Lord himself shall descend from heaven
with a shout, with the voice of the archangel,

**and with the trump of God: and the dead in
Christ shall rise first.** (1 Thess. 4:16)

The Lord Jesus himself will descend from heaven. He will leave
the *third heaven* to enter into our shadow planet's circle. This event
is portrayed to be a drop down into the "earth bubble," catch up his
saints, and then a quick retreat back into the *third heaven*. But there
are many passages that cause this interpretation to be problematic.
For instance, this passage in the book of Acts:

> *And he shall send Jesus Christ, which before was
> preached unto you: whom the heaven must receive
> until the times of restitution of all things, which
> God hath spoken by the mouth of all his holy proph-
> ets since the world began.* (Acts 3:20–21)

Unlike God the Father and the Holy Spirit, Jesus is housed in a
body, which is evident by his testimony in Luke:

> *Behold my hands and my feet, that it is I myself:
> handle me, and see; for a spirit hath not flesh and
> bones,* as ye see me have. (Luke 24:39)

He is located at a particular location, and according to scripture, it is in the third heaven. The second heaven is what we call outer
space.

> *So then after the Lord had spoken unto them, he
> was received up into heaven, and sat on the right
> hand of God.* (Mark 16:19)

The 1 Thessalonians 4:16 records that he would *descend* from
heaven (third heaven). If Jesus was still in the third heaven at the time
of the resurrection, there is no need to say that he would descend
from heaven. Peter proclaimed that the third heaven must receive
Jesus; that is, he must stay in the third heaven until it is time for the

restoration of all things, meaning the earth will be like it was before the fall in Eden. The lion would lie down with the lamb and so on (Isaiah 11:6, 65:25).

According to Acts 3:20–21, Jesus cannot leave the third heaven until he is ready to regenerate this shadowy earth. The restoration of the earth takes place during the millennial rein, which is the Day of the Lord. This regeneration is caused by the life-giving light of Jesus being present continually. When he appears, his light will destroy corruption and generate new life in the earth, restoring it as it was meant to be. This regeneration is evident by Jesus's statement to his disciples:

> *And Jesus said unto them, Verily I say unto you, That ye which have followed me, in the* regenera-tion *when the Son of man shall sit in the throne of his glory, ye also shall sit upon twelve thrones, judging the twelve tribes of Israel.* (Matt. 19:28)

Like the advancement of any kingdom, the kingdom of God will cause a war (Armageddon). Once that war is completed, the light of the Lord will cause amazing growth and prosperity to happen to Israel and to this planet, which will no longer have a shadow because of his light. This constitutes a problem for pre-tribulation and mid-tribulation viewpoints, which are named improperly because the tribulation starts in the middle of the seventieth week. Therefore, both viewpoints would be pre-tribulation. Jesus will not be able to enter our atmosphere until he is ready to restore the earth and reign as King of kings. With many of the viewpoints of the scripture, it is easy to let emotion or personal comfort influence the interpretation. The problem with allowing this to take place is that it can lead you to believe in error, which can squelch revelation and stunt your spiritual understanding and growth. Truth makes sense, and if you skip God's logic, you don't see his glory in its true perspective.

Now in reference to Jesus descending with a shout, the Old Testament prophets connect the voice or the shout of the Lord to this event described in 1 Thessalonians 4:16. Here are a few verses that make the connection between the Day of the Lord and the shout (1 Thess. 4:16).

> *God is gone up with a shout, the Lord with the sound of a trumpet.* (Ps. 47:5)

> *The Lord shall go forth as a mighty man, he shall stir up jealousy like a man of war:* he shall cry, yea, roar; he shall prevail against his enemies. *I have long time holden my peace; I have been still, and refrained myself:* now will I cry like a travailing woman; *I will destroy and devour at once.* (Isa. 42:13)

> *Therefore prophesy thou against them all these words, and say unto them, The Lord shall roar from on high, and* utter his voice *from his holy habitation; he shall mightily roar upon his habitation;* he shall give a shout, *as they that tread the grapes, against all the inhabitants of the earth.* (Jer. 25:30)

> *They shall walk after the Lord:* he shall roar like a lion: when he shall roar, then the children shall tremble from the west. (Hos. 11:10)

> *The great day of the Lord is near, it is near, and hasteth greatly,* even the voice of the day of the Lord: *the mighty man shall cry there bitterly.* (Zeph. 1:14)

> *The Lord also shall roar out of Zion,* and utter his voice *from Jerusalem; and the heavens and the earth shall shake: but the Lord will be the hope of his people, and the strength of the children of Israel.* (Joel 3:16)

And he said, The Lord will roar from Zion, *and utter his voice from Jerusalem; and the habitations of the shepherds shall mourn, and the top of Carmel shall wither.* (Amos 1:2)

Let's continue. (Bold type is our anchor scriptures.)

Then we which are alive and remain shall be caught up together with them in the clouds, to meet the Lord in the air: and so shall we ever be with the Lord. (1 Thess. 4:17).

This event of being "caught up" (*harpazo* in the Greek) together is labeled the rapture by many. Rapture does not appear in God's word, and the reason is God did not inspire it. It is a misunderstanding of the resurrection of the dead. Jesus is the resurrection, and he called himself just that.

Jesus said unto her, I am the resurrection, *and the life: he that believeth in me, though he were dead, yet shall he live.* (John 11:25)

Paul tells us that we are Christ's body:

Now ye are the body of Christ, and members in particular. (1 Cor. 12:27)

Let's look at a couple of passages that show how his body, after his resurrection, ascended.

And she brought forth a man child, who was to rule all nations with a rod of iron: and her child was caught up *unto God, and to his throne.* (Rev. 12:5)

Harpazo in this passage (meaning "caught up") is the same word that the Holy Spirit used to describe our ascension at the resurrection.

> *And when he had spoken these things, while they*
> *beheld, he was taken up; and a cloud received him*
> *out of their sight.* (Acts 1:9)

This passage about Jesus's ascension clearly shows that there were witnesses on the ground who beheld this event. The doctrine of the rapture is misleading. It twists the meaning of the resurrection. The word *rapture* originally meant to be "caught away" as one who has been transported thru a flash back memory in the mind (e.g., I was raptured back to the time when I was a child.). The resurrection, on the other hand, is a rising from the dead.

The rapture is thought of as a "twinkling of an eye" event. This is another misunderstanding. In order to understand the twinkling-of-an-eye passage, we must consider it closely to see what is really revealed.

> *Behold, I show you a mystery; We shall not all sleep,*
> but we shall all be changed. *In a moment, in the*
> twinkling of an eye, *at the last trump: for the*
> *trumpet shall sound, and the dead shall be raised*
> *incorruptible, and we shall be* changed. (1 Cor.
> 15:51–52)

As we can see by this passage, "in the twinkling of an eye, we shall be *changed.*" Being changed or resurrected at eye-blinking speed really doesn't have anything to do with the rate of ascension we will enjoy. The process or action is a conversion from flesh and blood to spiritual flesh and bone. The spirit gives life to our new celestial body. This body will have no blood. This is the reason Paul makes such a wonderful explanation as to the differences in the body we will receive.

God's glory will be amazing as he changes us from a terrestrial body into a celestial body in the twinkling of an eye. Much the same way, Jesus was resurrected, yet he did not leave the earth until he appeared to Mary (John 20:15–16). So the pattern is, we will be changed very quickly but ascend at a viewable speed. Furthermore, when Jesus returns, the book of Revelation records:

> *Behold, he cometh with clouds; and* every eye shall see him, *and they also which pierced him: and all kindreds of the earth shall wail because of him. Even so, Amen.* (Rev. 1:7)

Everyone will see him so traveling or ascending in the twinkling of an eye is in conflict with scripture. The reason they will be able to see him is heaven will come to earth. There will be no more veil between the two. His light will penetrate the earth all the way to the core, much like X-rays go through the body.

> ***Wherefore comfort one another with these words.*** (1 Thess. 4:18)

These words have been a comfort to many, especially during death and times of grief. Was Paul finished with his thought? No, sir! Why, you might ask? When Paul wrote this letter, it didn't have chapters and verses. It was on a scroll. Most of the time, this error of stopping with this passage is made when Paul's thoughts are much deeper. We must continue so we can understand this passage's meaning in full.

> ***But of the times and the seasons, brethren, ye have no need that I write unto you.*** (1 Thess. 5:1)

Chapter 5 starts with a conjunction, which is a word that connects thought. Paul is telling us that the times and seasons for the event of the Lord's descending with a shout, we have no need for him to write to us. Why?

> **For yourselves know** perfectly *that* **the day of the Lord** *so cometh as a thief in the night.* (1 Thess. 5:2)

Paul assumes that we understand *perfectly* the Old Testament concept of the Day of the Lord. He then clears up any doubt by connecting the event of the Lord descending with a shout on the Day of the Lord. Therefore, he is telling us that the resurrection takes place on the Day of the Lord, which takes place after the tribulation period as it is the last day (Sabbath) of this creation.

Let's go to Jesus himself with this question. He will bring light as to the timing of the resurrection. Jesus and I will now have a short conversation. "Jesus, when is it the Father's will for you to raise your people from the dead?"

> *And this is the* Father's will *which hath sent me, that of* all *which he hath given me, I should lose nothing, but should raise it up again at* the last day *(first witness).* (John 6:39, emphasis mine)

Jesus, let me see if I understand this right. You are saying that it is the Father's will (who sent you) that you raise *all* of us at *the last day.*

> *And this is the will of him that sent me, that* everyone *which seeth the Son, and believeth on him, may have everlasting life: and I will raise him up at* the last day *(second witness).* (John 6:40)

So you are saying that in order to be saved, God has to draw us and then you will resurrect us at the last day.

> *No man can come to me, except the Father which hath sent me draw him: and I will raise him up at* the last day *(third witness).* (John 6:44

Okay, my Lord. If I receive you as the Passover lamb and have communion with you, You will raise me up when?

> *Whoso eateth my flesh, and drinketh my blood, hath eternal life; and I will raise him up at* the last day *(fourth witness).* (John 6:54)

It is God's will to raise us up at the last day, not before or after. The Day of the Lord is the last day on this earth. Jesus, in the context of these passages, did not qualify this revelation to be the last day of a feast or any other Jewish event. He was simply talking about the last day of this creation with regard to the will of his Father. How do I know this, you may ask? Well, because when eternity starts, there will be no more days. The word *last* used in these passages in Greek is *eschatos*. Jesus tells us four times when it is God's will for us to be raise from the dead. The last day is a thousand-year day called the Day of the Lord. This day has a beginning (His coming to earth) and an ending (when Jesus ascends to the great white throne).

Now the word *raise*—or sometimes translated as "raised up"—used in these four verses in John chapter 6 is the same word used to describe Jesus's resurrection in Acts, *"This Jesus hath God raised up, whereof we all are witnesses"* (Acts 2:32). Jesus is talking resurrection being raised from the dead, not rapture, which also includes transportation and removal from earth. In addition, the raising from the dead always involves witnesses. This foreshadowing truth of this last day resurrection is revealed in the passage about the celebration of the feast of tabernacles. The feast of the tabernacles is a seven-day feast which was celebrated in the wilderness. This feast acknowledges the time of harvest. When Jesus walked among men here on earth, the Bible records that he celebrated this feast.

> *In the* last day, *that great day of the feast, Jesus stood and* cried, *saying, If any man thirst, let him come unto me, and drink.* (John 7:37)

There is lots of revelation in this verse pertaining to the Day of the Lord and resurrection contain therein:

1. We notice that it was the last day of a seven-day feast. This event points to the Sabbath day, which is our day of rest after the end of a seven-thousand-year cycle.
2. It is the last day, which coincides with the truth of the harvest of the earth.
3. Jesus stands up, which shows that he will stand at his Father's right hand.
4. He cries out, which is a shout to gain the attention of the ones present to hear him. Remember that the Lord descends from heaven with a shout. He will have to stand because he is seated at his Father's right hand.
5. He says to come to him if any man thirsts. I don't know about you, but I am thirsty to take off this earthly man suit which is this tabernacle.

The giving of the living water (Holy Spirit), shows the shedding of this terrestrial body or tabernacle and the putting on a celestial body. This is the sign of our life force after resurrection. God's Word is amazing! Let's continue with this passage in 1 Thessalonians:

> *For when they shall say, Peace and safety; then sudden destruction cometh upon them, as travail upon a woman with child; and they shall not escape.* (1 Thess. 5:3)

This passage is showing Israel will not recognize that Jesus is the Lord until the time of tribulation. These birth pains described by Jesus in Matthew, Mark, and Luke will happen just before the Day of the Lord dawns.

> *But ye, brethren, are not in darkness, that that day should overtake you as a thief.* (1 Thess. 5:4)

Why will we not be overtaken as a thief? Because we understand what the Day of the Lord is. Now as we discussed earlier after the tribulation when the sun goes out, this is why he comes as a thief in the night. If the sun was still shining on any part of the earth, then Jesus could not come as a thief in the night. Why, you ask? Because in the solar system, Earth is always part light and part dark. If Jesus were to come while the sun is the light of the world, some part of the world would not be in darkness. Therefore, his statement would only be partly true. It is amazing to me that every word recorded in the Bible is so precise. We could not understand this until we found out that Earth is orbiting the sun.

> *Ye are all the children of light, and the children of the day: we are not of the night, nor of darkness.* (1 Thess. 5:5)

When resurrected on the Day of the Lord, we will shine like the sun (Matt. 13:43). Furthermore, Paul calls us children of the Day, referring to the fact that we are resurrected from the grave, literally born from the dead as children of His day. Revelation 20:5 says, "*But the rest of the dead lived not again until the thousand years were finished. This is the* first resurrection.*"*

As we discussed in chapter 2 the thousand years noted in Revelation 20, is the Day of the Lord, and verse 5 boldly declares that this is the *first resurrection.* First means there is none before it. The resurrection is the harvest of the earth. God is going to reap the souls Jesus redeemed, and the harvest is the resurrection. As Paul stated in:

> *But every man in his own order: Christ* the first fruits; *afterward they that are Christ's at* his coming. (1 Cor. 15:23)

Paul is reminding us of the law of first fruits as spoken in Exodus 23:

> *The first of the first fruits of thy land thou shalt bring into the house of the Lord thy God.* (Exod. 23:19)

This is the pattern. Christ has risen from the dead, being the first fruits of the harvest. As the Old Testament teaches, the first fruits are God's. Then those who are in Christ will be resurrected at his coming. This is the harvest of the earth (His body, the wheat).

> *And another angel came out of the temple, crying with a loud voice to him that sat on the cloud, Thrust in thy sickle, and reap: for the time is come for thee to reap; for the harvest of the earth is ripe.* (Rev. 14:15)

Also reflected in the interpretation of the wheat and tares:

> **Let both grow together until the harvest: and in the time of harvest I will say to the reapers, Gather ye together first the tares, and bind them in bundles to burn them: but gather the wheat into my barn.** (Matt. 13:30)

Interpretation:

> **He answered and said unto them, He that soweth the good seed is the Son of man; The field is the world; the good seed are the children of the kingdom; but the tares are the children of the wicked one; The enemy that sowed them is the devil; the harvest is the end of the world; and the reapers are the angels.** (Matt. 13:37–39)

The end of the world is referring to the end of the prince of the power of the air (Satan), whose dominion is during the current solar system. Also noted in the book of Daniel, *"But go thou thy way till the end be: for thou shalt rest, and stand in thy lot at the end of the days"* (Dan. 12:13). Daniel was standing on his lot, the piece of land allotted to his tribe. The *end of days* is once again referring to the death of the solar system and the resurrection of the dead. When the sun is no longer shining, then the cycle of twelve-hour days or end of days is accomplished.

In the book of Job it is made clear that we cannot be raised until the heavens (solar system) are gone.

> *But man dieth, and wasteth away: yea, man giveth up the ghost, and where is he? As the waters fail from the sea, and the flood decayeth and drieth up: So man lieth down, and riseth not: till the heavens be no more, they shall not awake, nor be raised out of their sleep. (Job 14:10–12 KJV)*

In Matthew 28, when Jesus gives us the great commission, this truth is revealed:

> *Go ye therefore, and teach all nations, baptizing them in the name of the Father, and of the Son, and of the Holy Ghost: Teaching them to observe all things whatsoever I have commanded you: and, lo, I am with you always, even unto the end of the world. Amen.*

In the book of Hebrews chapter 11, there is a list of many of those who lived by faith, but I want to focus on verses 35–40 because there is a statement in verse 40 that can easily be overlook, losing its meaning.

> *Women received their dead raised to life again: and others were tortured, not accepting deliverance; that they might obtain a better resurrection: And*

*others had trial of cruel mockings and scourgings,
yea, moreover of bonds and imprisonment: They
were stoned, they were sawn asunder, were tempted,
were slain with the sword: they wandered about in
sheepskins and goatskins; being destitute, afflicted,
tormented; (Of whom the world was not worthy:)
they wandered in deserts, and in mountains, and
in dens and caves of the earth. And these all, having obtained a good report through faith,* received
not the promise*: God having provided some better
thing for us, that they* without us should not be
made perfect. (Heb. 11:35–40)*

Even after all the afflictions and torments, the Old Testament
saints suffered. God would not let them be made perfect (resurrected)
without us. Why? Because you cannot resurrect part of Christ's body.
We are saved people. In Christ, the spirit and soul have been regen-
erated, but the body is still dying because of sin. To be made perfect
is the resurrection of a new body.

This proves that God is no respecter of persons. Abraham,
Isaac, and Jacob are part of the church. In fact, they entered "the
church" (*ecclesia*) before we did. It is easy to think that the church
and the New Testament were created at the same time, but the truth
is the church was created with the covenant of Abraham. The church
was empowered at Pentecost. Apostle Peter was a Jewish believer
and preached at Pentecost. There were no Gentiles inducted into
the church. This is evident by Cornelius the Centurion becoming a
believer in Acts chapter 10 and their astonishment when the Holy
Ghost was given to the Gentiles.

*While Peter yet spake these words, the Holy Ghost
fell on all them which heard the word. And they
of the circumcision which believed were astonished,
as many as came with Peter, because that on the
Gentiles also was poured out the gift of the Holy
Ghost.*

The Bible records that the Jewish believers were acknowledge as the church five times before Acts chapter 10. God did this because salvation was given to the Jews first. He didn't want us to make the mistake we are making in saying that the church is made up of Gentile believers only. Jesus grafted the Gentiles into Israel. So the Old Testament saints could not be made perfect without the New Testament saints as the rest of his body. This means there can be no partial resurrection.

This is reflected in Jesus statement in the Gospel according to John, *"And other sheep I have, which are not of this fold: them also I must bring, and they shall hear my voice; and there shall be one fold, and one shepherd"* (John 10:16). The fold is the whole house of Israel, and the shepherd is Jesus. This is what Ezekiel is talking about when the Valley of the Dry Bones are resurrected, *"Then he said unto me, Son of man,* these bones are the whole house of Israel*: behold, they say, Our bones are dried, and our hope is lost: we are cut off for our parts"* (Ezek. 37:11).

Let's look at another passage that is about the resurrection and how it is connected to the day of the Lord.

> *Arise, shine;* for thy light is come, *and the glory of the Lord is risen upon thee.* (Isa. 60:1)

In this passage, we see the resurrection in the first word *arise.* We arise because our *light has come.* The Day of the Lord (Christ) is shining in the glory of his Farther, and he has risen as the sun of righteousness upon us, the children and adopted children of Israel. Isaiah 60:2 says, *"For, behold, the darkness shall cover the earth, and gross darkness the people: but the Lord shall arise upon thee, and his glory shall be seen upon thee."*

The "darkness shall cover the earth" is referring to the Day of the Lord coming as a thief in the night. This is because the sun has been forever darkened by the shaking of the solar system. *Gross darkness* is referring to the fact that spiritual wickedness is running rampant on earth. The sun, moon, and stars will be darkened, but the Lord will arise like the sun. His glory will be seen by all. His day will dawn upon the children of the day, those who are born from the grave on that day.

"I tell you, in that night there shall be two men in one bed; the one shall be taken, and the other shall be left," says Luke 17:34. This passage gives a dilemma for pre-tribulation and mid-tribulation views. How can the phrase "in that night" be true for everyone while the sun is still shinning? For some parts of the earth, it would still be day because the sun would still be shining. Is this passage completely true or not? The sun is not shining because the solar system has been shaken apart when Jesus comes like a thief in the night.

After Jesus spoke these passages, the disciples asked him where this would take place. Now notice they did not ask him when, but where:

> *And they answered and said unto him,* Where, *Lord? And he said unto them, Wheresoever the body is, thither will the eagles be gathered together.* (Luke 17:37)

The eagles or vultures that Jesus was referring too are the same birds that the angel calls to the supper of our great God:

> *And I saw an angel standing in the sun; and he cried with a loud voice, saying to all the* fowls *that fly in the midst of heaven, Come and gather your-selves together unto the supper of the great God. That ye may eat the flesh of kings, and the flesh of captains, and the flesh of mighty men, and the flesh of horses, and of them that sit on them, and the flesh of all men, both free and bond, both small and great.* (Rev. 19:17–18).

Paul further explains to us the timing of the resurrection in 2 Thessalonians 2:1, *"Now we beseech you, brethren, by the coming of our Lord Jesus Christ, and* by our gathering together unto him." In this verse, Paul is pleading with us by Jesus's coming and our resurrection. We will be resurrected and gather unto him. *"That ye be not soon shaken in mind, or be troubled, neither by spirit, nor by word, nor by letter as from us,* as that the day of Christ is at hand*"* (2 Thess. 2:2). Paul is speaking words of comfort because at this time, there were rumors that Jesus had already come, and fear of missing his coming was a major concern. This fear promoted today is the same fear in the phrase "left behind." God does not leave his children behind. Paul wants us not to be shaken in mind or troubled by spirit or by words because the source of these rumors did not originate from him regarding the day of Christ.

"Let no man deceive you by any means: for that day *shall not come, except there come a falling away first, and that man of sin be revealed, the son of perdition"* (2 Thess. 2:3). Paul explains in this verse two things that are restraining Jesus from appearing. First, there has to be a defection from the truth. This is commonly thought of as a loss of attendance in the church. However, Paul is revealing to us that true devotion to Christ will be lost. This really doesn't have anything to do with church attendance. Second is that the son of perdition must take his place in history. Now there is a lot of speculation as to who that is. It is clearly seen in the scripture who he is, but that is for another book. Paul tells us not to let men deceive us by any means because he knows that the pre-tribulation, mid-tribulation, or any other false doctrines or viewpoints will be coming to deceive us in the day before our Savior comes.

> *For, behold,* the day cometh, *that shall burn as an oven; and all the proud, yea, and all that do wickedly, shall be stubble: and the day that cometh shall burn them up, saith the Lord of hosts, that it shall leave them neither root nor branch. But unto you that fear my name shall the* Sun *of righteousness arise with healing in his wings; and ye shall go forth, and grow up as calves of the stall.* (Mal. 4:1–2)

Notice that the light of the Lord destroys everything that is impure. We must be ready to meet him. Sun of righteousness refers to Jesus taking the place of the sun as the light of the world. Also, arise with healing is referring to the fact that he is the Sabbath day, no doubt the woman with the issue of blood knew this passage well; because she knew the wings of his garment had healing in them. Wings also can refer to rays of light. Psalm 84:11 says, *"For the Lord God is a sun and shield: the Lord will give grace and glory: no good thing will he withhold from them that walk uprightly."*

This passage is declaring that our God, who is expressed in Jesus, is a sun, not the sun of our solar system but the source of brilliance to sustain life on earth:

> *Moreover the light of the moon shall be as the light of the sun, and the light of the sun shall be sevenfold, as the light of seven days,* in the day *that the Lord bindeth up the breach of his people, and healeth the stroke of their wound.* (Isaiah 30:26)

This passage is awesome! It shows how much brighter his light is than our current sun. In order to understand the context, the sun in this passage is referring to God himself. Since our current sun shall darkened after the tribulation, God's light will be shining as powerful as seven suns because it is seven times brighter than our current sun. Jesus is the seventh day (the Sabbath), and seven is the number of perfection. God's light will be shining in all its perfection during his day. He is also seven times brighter because the moon will be reflecting that light, which will be as bright as our current sun.

According to Luke 17:24, *"For as the lightning, that lighteneth out of the one part under heaven, shineth unto the other part under heaven; so shall also the Son of man be in his day."* This passage is showing how that the Day of the Lord is the Son of Man's day. Jesus's day, the brightness of his luminance, is comparable to lightning.

The final evidence I want to offer will synch the time of the resurrection and show a legality that must take place before the resurrection can even take place.

In a moment, in the twinkling of an eye, **at the last trump***: for the trumpet shall sound, and the dead shall be raised incorruptible, and we shall be changed.* (1 Cor. 15:52)

Seven trumpets sound in the book of Revelation. I want to look at what happens during the last one. Understand that a trumpet's blast accomplishes certain tasks. It can announce a king, sound an alarm for proclamation purposes, or call a gathering of the people. All three is what this trumpet does. The seventh trumpet is the last trumpet ever to sound for these purposes. The Holy Spirit will connect us after this trumpet, and we will never wonder what is going on ever again. Praise his name! So let's look at what happens at this trumpet.

And the seventh angel sounded; and there were great voices in heaven, saying, The kingdoms of this world are become the kingdoms of our Lord, and of his Christ; and he shall reign for ever and ever. (Rev. 11:15)

The first thing that happens after this trumpet blast is a proclamation—not just any proclamation, one the most important ones to ever to take place. Jesus takes possession of the shadow planet. This is a legal seizing of this earth. Now Jesus comes to earth like a thief in the night, but that is how he comes as, not what he comes to do. He is claiming what he purchased at Calvary. Jesus told Pontius Pilate at his trial, "but now is my kingdom not from hence". (John 18) His position at the trumpet has officially changed. Why is this so important to the resurrection? It's because he had to legally take possession before he can eternally resurrect. We must understand just how important for God to do everything right.

And the four and twenty elders, which sat before God on their seats, fell upon their faces, and worshipped God, Saying, We give thee thanks, O Lord God Almighty, which art, and wast, and art to come; because thou hast taken to thee thy great power, and hast reigned. 18 And the nations were angry, and thy wrath is come, and the time of the dead, that they should be judged, and that thou shouldest give reward unto thy servants the prophets, and to the saints, and them that fear thy name, small and great; and shouldest destroy them which destroy the earth. (Rev. 11:16–18)

In verse 18, there is a careful and precise list of reasons this trumpet was blown, let's look.

1. The nations are "angry" was foretold in Psalm 2.
2. "Thy wrath is come" is speaking of God's righteous indignation that will result in Armageddon.
3. "Time of the dead" is referring to the resurrection of the dead. With this trumpet, the first resurrection will take place. The only resurrection that will take place in which the second death will no longer have power. This is the last trumpet ever to be blow that will gather the church, his body, from Abraham to the last star of faith that was promised to him as he gazed into the sky when God said "so shall thy seed be." There are two kinds of seed to Abraham, the stars of the sky and the sands of the sea. These starry seeds are judged righteous because of the blood of the Lamb and the word of their testimony. This is the reward of his servants—prophets, saints, and those who fear his name.
4. Armageddon is coming. God will take retribution on those attempting to destroy his earth.

I would like to offer a couple more passages that will bring us to the same conclusion that Jesus is the Day of the Lord. His second coming is the time of the resurrection, rest, and Sabbath of creation, as stated in Mathew chapter 25.

Then shall the kingdom of heaven be likened unto ten virgins, which took their lamps, and went forth to meet the bridegroom. And five of them were wise, and five were foolish. They that were foolish took their lamps, and took no oil with them: But the wise took oil in their vessels with their lamps. While the bridegroom tarried, they all slumbered and slept. And at midnight there was a cry made, *Behold, the bridegroom cometh; go ye out to meet him. Then all those virgins arose, and trimmed their lamps. And the foolish said unto the wise, Give us of your oil; for our lamps are gone out. But the wise answered, saying, Not so; lest there be not enough for us and you: but go ye rather to them that sell, and buy for yourselves. And while they went to buy, the bridegroom came; and they that were ready went in with him to the marriage: and the door was shut.* Afterward came also the other virgins, saying, Lord, Lord, open to us. *But he answered and said, Verily I say unto you, I know you not.* (Matt. 25:1–12)

So we know this story to be the parable of the ten virgins. I would like to point out that this parable is pointing out some very interesting points we have already discussed that further support the Day of the Lord. First of all, in verse 6, Jesus says that the cry or shout (1 Thess. 4:16) is made at midnight. Now it is really easy to discount what Jesus is saying here unless you understand the Day of the Lord. If you understand the Day of the Lord as we have discussed it, you will realize that when Jesus returns, the Sun will be extinguished (darkened). The power of this truth is far reaching. This means that when Jesus descends with a shout, it will be midnight or blackest part of night on the whole planet. It truly will be midnight for everyone on planet Earth. You see, what makes God's word so amazing is the fact that it is true in every sense of the word. Another point I want to make is contained in verse 11. If the door is in heaven, then how do the other virgins come and talk to the Lord later by asking him to open the door? In other words, they would have to ascend up to heaven or the door has to be here on earth. The door will be here on Earth.

I am going to show you a mystery that, if you have been a Bible student at all, you may have run across this passage and didn't even have a clue what it meant. Once I show you then it will be clear what this passage means in verse 11 of Matthew 25.

> *And Jesus said unto them, Can the* children of the bridechamber *mourn, as long as the bridegroom is with them? but the days will come, when the bridegroom shall be taken from them, and then shall they fast.* (Matt. 9:15).

Why didn't Jesus's disciples fast? We are supposed to fast, but it is the way Jesus answer the question perfectly that I would like for you to focus on. *"Can the children of the bridechamber mourn as long as the bridegroom is with them"* is talking about the born-again children of God. The question is, where is the bridechamber? Is it in heaven or on earth? The answer is on earth. Remember the testimony of Jesus is the spirit of prophecy. So where does the word of God tell us that this chamber is going to be located? It is in a passage that you have never heard preached because without the Day of the Lord revelation, you can't understand it since the events are located within this glorious day.

> In that day *shall the branch of the Lord be beautiful and glorious, and the fruit of the earth shall be excellent and comely for them that are escaped of Israel. And it shall come to pass, that he that is left in Zion, and he that remaineth in Jerusalem, shall be called holy, even every one that is written among the living in Jerusalem: When the Lord shall have washed away the filth of the daughters of Zion, and shall have purged the blood of Jerusalem from the midst thereof by the spirit of judgment, and by*

> *the spirit of burning. And the Lord will create upon
> every dwelling place of mount Zion, and upon her
> assemblies, a cloud and smoke by day, and the shin-
> ing of a flaming fire by night: for upon all the glory
> shall be a* defence. (Isa. 4:2–5)

Upon the Mountain of Zion during the Day of the Lord, God will create upon all the glory that is the illumination of his person and those who are resurrected shining like the sun, a defence. The Hebrew word for defence is *chuppah*, which means "chamber." So in the day of the Lord—or as Isaiah calls it, "in that day"—the Lord Jesus will be beautiful and glorious and will protect the children in a bridechamber. The door will be shut when those foolish virgins will come knocking.

The second passage I would like to point out is the very testimony of our Lord himself:

> *But Jesus held his peace. And the high priest answered
> and said unto him, I adjure thee by the living God,
> that thou tell us whether thou be the Christ, the Son
> of God. Jesus saith unto him, Thou hast said: nev-
> ertheless I say unto you,* Hereafter shall ye see the
> Son of man sitting on the right hand of power,
> and coming in the clouds of heaven. (Matt.
> 26.63–64)

During the trial when Jesus was brought before the Sanhedrin, the high priest pressed Jesus to answer, "Are you the Christ the Son of God?" Jesus told the high priest that he himself would see Jesus in two places. One as his judge who was setting on the right hand of power, no doubt after the priest's death. The second time is when the Day of the Lord is revealed during Jesus's second coming. When Jesus is revealed from heaven, every eye will see him, even those who pierced him.

Behold, he cometh with clouds; and every eye shall see him, and they also which pierced him*: and all kindreds of the earth shall wail because of him. Even so, Amen.* (Rev. 1:7)

So since we are resurrected on the Day of the Lord (Christ), we can see Paul's rejoicing and understand his statements fully. Paul new that once we resurrect, his labor in the gospel was not in vain.

Being confident of this very thing, that he which hath begun a good work in you will perform it until the day of Jesus Christ. (Phil. 1:6)

That ye may approve things that are excellent; that ye may be sincere and without offence till the day of Christ. (Phil. 1:10)

"Holding forth the word of life; that I may rejoice in the day of Christ, that I have not run in vain, *neither laboured in vain"* (Phil. 2:16).

Who shall also confirm you unto the end, that ye may be blameless in the day of our Lord Jesus Christ. (1 Cor. 1:8)

To deliver such an one unto Satan for the destruction of the flesh, that the spirit may be saved in the day of the Lord Jesus. (1 Cor. 5:5)

As also ye have acknowledged us in part, that we are your rejoicing, even as ye also are ours in the day of the Lord Jesus. (2 Cor. 1:14)

Henceforth there is laid up for me a crown of righteousness, which the Lord, the righteous judge, shall give me at that day: *and not to me only, but unto all them also that love his appearing.* (2 Tim. 4:8)

This is further evidence for the resurrection on the Day of the Lord. If the resurrection of the dead is going to happen before or during the tribulation, why wait for the Day of the Lord to rejoice about it? The Day of the Lord is the Sabbath of creation, the seventh thousand-year day.

This is the reason for so many references to the resurrection—the cleansing or rest from problems—happening on the Sabbath day. This is all reveling who Jesus is, the Omega (last), the Lord of the Sabbath, the healer, the warrior, the completion, and the seven spirits of God.

- Enoch was the seventh from Adam (showing a new spiritual life).
- Joshua (Jesus) fought the battle of Jericho, circling and blowing trumpets for seven days with seven blasts.
- The priest sprinkled blood seven times for sin and healing.
- The child Elijah raised from the dead sneezed seven times.
- The punishment for sin was seven times over in Leviticus.
- Psalm 12:6 declares that God's Word (Jesus) is like silver (redemption) tried in a furnace seven times.
- Naaman the leper had to dip seven times in the Jordan, the same river Jesus got baptized in.
- The seventy weeks in Daniel.
- All the times Jesus healed people on the Sabbath.

All of these examples are pointing to who Jesus is, the resurrection, the Sabbath, and the Day (light) of the Lord.

Let's sum up this chapter. Every verse in the Bible will take you to the same conclusion. I have looked for over thirty years and have never found a verse that contradicts this truth. Jesus is the resurrection, and the resurrection will take place on the last day. The Day of the Lord, which is the Sabbath day of this creation, is when we are raised as the children of light and day. The Day of the Lord comes as thief in the night because the sun is replaced by the Son!

When Will His Day Dawn?

*But of that day and hour knoweth no man, no, not
the angels of heaven, but my Father only.*
—Matthew 24:36

It is apparent by this verse that we cannot pinpoint the *day and hour* that the Day of the Lord will dawn, unlike Jesus's first coming (Daniel chapter 9). We are not able to calculate it to a certain day. That is to the time of Palm Sunday (the first day of the week) when Jesus presented himself as the Messiah riding on a donkey. But we also can't go in the opposite direction and say there is no way of knowing a general time frame of his return. After all, he said the *day and hour* could not be known. The hours or minutes of his return is not revealed to us, nor will be revealed to any man, God said. What can we know about the his return? Has he left us in complete darkness about the dawning of his day?

Let me show you what he revealed to me in the light of the Day of the Lord revelation that will narrow the time frame down to an understandable season. Understand that I am not picking a day or hour. With that being said, let's look at some interesting evidence that will show you just how close the day is. We will start this journey in the book of Hosea where God required Hosea to take a wife that was a whore (Gomer). God did this to show what he had to suffer when dealing with the children of Israel.

> ***The beginning of the word of the Lord by Hosea. And the Lord said to Hosea, Go, take unto thee a wife of whoredoms and children of whoredoms: for the land hath committed great whoredom, departing from the Lord.*** (Hos 1:2)

After Hosea takes his wife and they have their first child, God tells Hosea to name him *Jezreel*, which means "God sows" in Hebrew. This is a revelation that Jesus the light is going to be born or sown through Israel, Abraham's descendants. Hosea then has two more children. The next one was a girl named Lo-ruhamah, meaning "no mercy," which shows what God would allow to happen to the nation who rejects his Son. This happened to Israel from the time of their rejection until the time of their acceptance of him during the final week of Daniel's chapter 9 prophecies. God showed no mercy by allowing the Romans to crucified thousands and scattered them throughout the earth. Hitler then killed millions in his gas chambers without mercy. Jesus prophesied of this when he said, *"But Jesus turning unto them said, Daughters of Jerusalem,* weep not for me, but weep for yourselves, and for your children" (Luke 23:28).

Hosea then had a son he named Loammi, which means "not my people," which is what happen also at the rejection of Jesus. Jesus showing this by sayings, *"Therefore say I unto you, The kingdom of God shall be taken from you, and given to a nation bringing forth the fruits thereof"* (Matt. 21:43).

With this proclamation, the Jews fulfilled their purpose in the gospel plan of being the sowers as Hosea's first child reveals. Israel was blinded to the seed after they sowed it so that the Gentiles adopted by Christ could enter God's plan as reapers of the harvest "that is bringing forth the fruits." He then scattered his people to the four winds of heaven until they realize who Jesus is.

Israel is the sower and Gentiles as the reapers—this theme is God's plan so that both Jews (Israel) and Gentiles (the nations) would have a part of the redemption plan and can rejoice together at Christ's return. It is important to know this so that we can understand his plan and the fact that the Day of the Lord is right on schedule. Now knowing that Israel is the sower and the Gentiles are the reapers and we are not ignorant of the fact that a Day with the Lord is as a thousand years, we understand a large revelation about the return of Jesus.

> *When Ephraim saw his sickness, and Judah saw his wound, then went Ephraim to the Assyrian, and sent to king Jareb: yet could he not heal you, nor cure you of your wound.* (Hos. 5:13)

The northern tribes, alluded to here by the name Ephraim, went to the Assyrians to be healed instead of going to God. Therefore, God used Assyria to scatter these tribes to the four winds because they put their trust in men instead of God. The center of the Bible says, *"It is better to trust in the Lord than to put confidence in man"* (Ps. 118:8). This is the meaning of life, trust in God instead of yourself.

The passage of scripture that tells of this, *"Until the Lord removed Israel out of his sight, as he had said by all his servants the prophets. So was Israel carried away out of their own land to Assyria unto this day"* (2 Kgs. 17:23).

> *For I will be unto Ephraim as a lion, and as a young lion to the house of Judah: I, even I, will tear and go away; I will take away, and none shall rescue him.* (Hos. 5:14)

When Jesus was presented to the southern kingdom (Judah), they rejected him, and he responded by saying

> *O Jerusalem, Jerusalem, thou that killest the prophets, and stonest them which are sent unto thee, how often would I have gathered thy children together, even as a hen gathereth her chickens under her*

wings, and ye would not! Behold, your house is left unto you desolate. (Matt. 23:37–38)

Jesus is revealing the young lion tearing Judah, which took place in Jerusalem AD 70 by the Romans.

I will go and return to my place, till they acknowledge their offence, and seek my face: in their affliction they will seek me early. (Hos. 5:15)

I have often read this passage and did not understand its meaning until it was time. Then this verse opened up, and I saw what it was talking about. First of all, God revealed himself to Israel as the pillar of fire when they came out of the land of Egypt, at Mount Sinai with the giving of the Law, and in the holy of holies in Solomon's temple. These took place in the past before Hosea was written so when He says "I will go and return to my place," He isn't referring to these manifestations.

The only other time that God revealed himself to his people is when he became flesh and walked among them. Then I understood that "returning to my place" is referring to the ascension of Jesus when the Son of God took his place at the Father's right hand. Jesus will not return until after Israel acknowledges their offence as a nation. That will not take place until early in the tribulation period, which is the last half (forty-two months) of the seventieth week of Daniel's prophecy. This is when they will seek his face and in their affliction (tribulation).

This is reflected in the book of Revelation, *"And she brought forth a man child, who was to rule all nations with a rod of iron: and her child was caught up unto God, and to his throne"* (Rev. 12:5). When the woman (Israel) brought forth the child Jesus (the seed) who was to rule all nations with a rod of iron, her child was caught up (the ascension) unto God and to his throne. This took place in AD 32 with the ascension of Jesus, *"And the woman fled into the wilderness, where she hath a place prepared of God that they should feed her there a thousand two hundred and threescore days"* (Rev. 12:6).

During the tribulation, Hosea was referring to and is why we jump from Jesus's ascension to the early part of the tribulation period. Just as Hosea prophesied in chapter 5 and as Revelation 12 with the woman fleeing into the wilderness, which also agrees with the Olivet Discourse in Matthew 24.

In addition, the book of Revelation chapters 4 through 19, details Daniel's seventieth week prophecy. God also points out that this is going to happen in the book of Micah chapter 5, the vary passage that tells of Jesus's first coming, *"But thou, Bethlehem Ephratah, though thou be little among the thousands of Judah, yet out of thee shall he come forth unto me that is to be ruler in Israel; whose goings forth have been from of old, from everlasting"* (Mic. 5:2). This part of the prophecy tells of his first coming, *"Therefore will he give them up, until the time that she which travaileth hath brought forth: then the remnant of his brethren shall return unto the children of Israel"* (Mic. 5:3). This verse says the same story that Hosea is telling about Israel in the tribulation period, which is their time to be born again. It is very important to realize that Gentiles are not the replacement for Israel, but were given the opportunity to enter into God's plan. The church or gathering of citizens is rooted in Israel,. *"And he shall stand and feed in the strength of the Lord, in the majesty of the name of the Lord his God; and they shall abide: for now shall he be great unto the ends of the earth"* (Mic. 5:4).

Okay, now that we know that returning to my place referred to in the ascension, we can look at the next chapter to get a feel for the time of his return.

Come, and let us return unto the Lord: for he hath torn, and he will heal us; he hath smitten, and he will bind us up. (Hos. 6:1)

The prophet Hosea starts this chapter with a plea, "Come, and let us return to the Lord" because he has torn, in Jerusalem AD 70. He (Jesus) will heal us, smite us, and bind us up. They will seek him early in the tribulation period. But the healing of the nation of Israel will not take place until they see Jesus return. They weep for him. This is noted in Zechariah:

> *And I will pour upon the house of David, and upon the inhabitants of Jerusalem, the spirit of grace and of supplications: and they shalllook upon me whom they have pierced, and they shall mourn for him, as one mourneth for his only son, and shall be in bitterness for him, as one that is in bitterness for his firstborn.* (Zech. 12:10)

Here is the key verse as to when the season of his return will take place:

> **After two days will he revive us: in the third day he will raise us up, and we shall live in his sight.** (Hos. 6:2)

Now we know his ascension happened around AD 32. In addition, because we are not ignorant that a day with the Lord is as a thousand years and a thousand years as a day, these verses would place his return somewhere around AD 2032. After the two days, which are equal to two thousand years or two days in the Lord's perspective. Then he will raise us up in the resurrection that takes place of the last day (the Day of the Lord), the seventh day from creation yet the third day from the ascension.

Now before you start to panic, remember this is just an observation from the scripture. I am saying this fits the period Hosea is prophesying about, and it is very interesting and near. After this, I started to see if these *two days* were showing up anywhere else. Much to my surprise, I found several things. We just discussed the fact that Israel was the sower and the Gentiles are the reapers. The thought occurred to me that I am a Gentile adopted as Paul wrote, grafted into Israel's olive tree (Rom. 11:17, 24). This would make me part Jew by adoption (to the tribe of Judah) and part Gentile by natural birth. I remembered what is written in the gospel of John chapter 4. As we look at John 4, keep in mind that the Samaritans were part Jew and part Gentile. This is why the Jews wouldn't have anything to do with them because they were a mixed breed. This mixing of the Jews and Gentiles was foretold in the Old Testament in many places and stories. Just a couple examples of these are below:

> *And he said, It is a light thing that thou shouldest be my servant to raise up the tribes of Jacob, and to restore the preserved of Israel: I will also give thee for a light to the Gentiles, that thou mayest be my salvation unto the end of the earth.* (Isa. 49:6)

> *Ask of me, and I shall give thee the heathen for thine inheritance, and the uttermost parts of the earth for thy possession.* (Ps. 2:8)

This mixing of the Jews and Gentiles was also spoken of by Paul and is a running theme throughout the New Testament.

> *But now in Christ Jesus ye who sometimes were far off are made nigh by the blood of Christ. For he is our peace, who hath made both one, and hath broken down the middle wall of partition between us; Having abolished in his flesh the enmity, even the law of commandments contained in ordinances; for to make in himself of twain* one new man, *so making peace; And that he might reconcile both unto God in one body by the cross, having slain the enmity thereby.* (Eph. 2:13)

In John chapter 4, Jesus met a Samaritan woman at Jacob's well. Jesus had a conversation with her about the living water, who we should worship, and the correct location of worship. When the woman asked Jesus for the living water, Jesus asked her to go call her husband. She replied, "I do not have a husband." Jesus said, "You are telling the truth because you have already had five husbands, and the one you are currently living with is not your husband." This surprised the women, and she went back into the city telling everyone that Jesus was there and that she believed that he was the Messiah. She became a believer. Jesus would be her seventh husband, spiritually speaking, during her eternal rest, her Sabbath.

When Jesus's disciples came back with the food and asked him to eat, Jesus said to them:

> *Say not ye, There are yet four months, and then cometh harvest? behold, I say unto you, Lift up your eyes, and look on the fields; for they are white already to harvest. And he that reapeth receiveth wages, and gathereth fruit unto life eternal: that both he that soweth and he that reapeth may rejoice together.* (John 4:35-36)

There are two points that I want to focus on regarding the two-day issue that we discussed earlier in Hosea. The first aspect is to keep in mind that Jesus is interacting with a race of people who are both Jews and Gentiles, which is a type and shadow of Gentile believers grafted into Israel (Eph. 2:12–14). The first point is Jesus is here with the reapers (Jewish Gentiles) and in the above verses (John 4:35–36). He is revealing to his disciples God's plan, which is that the Jews are the sowers of the seed (Jesus) and Gentiles are reapers of the harvest. He quotes:

> *And herein is that saying true, One soweth (Jews), and another reapeth (Gentiles).* (John 4:37; emphasis added)

Now when the women returns with the first harvest of souls from the gospel, they ask Jesus to abide with them, and he chooses to do so for *two days*.

*So when the Samaritans were come unto him,
they besought him that he would tarry with
them: and he abode there two days.* (John 4:40)

The second point I want you to ponder is that God's word is a
revelation, not a coincidence. Each word written was inspired, and
each event was set up by divine appointment. Jesus tarried with the
Samaritans for two days to illustrate that God's plan now focused
on the Gentiles for the start of the reaping process, which continues
for two thousand years (two divine days). Jesus, who is divine, knew
that the Jews would reject him then seek him early in the tribulation
(affliction) period, and that he would resurrect them after the two
days. Jesus knew he would return to his place and oversee the task
of reaping until the times of the Gentiles were complete, which will
take two divine days or two thousand years of earth time (first New
Testament witness of the two days). Keep in mind that Jesus himself
was in the earth for two days and arose on the third day. We are his
body. As the head goes, so goes the body.

This pattern plays out again in a different story about the Good
Samaritan. In this story, Jesus is answering the question from a certain lawyer in Luke 10:25, "Who is my neighbor?" Jesus tells of a
man who fell among thieves and left "half dead." The state that we
are in, as born-again Christians, our spirits are alive and our flesh is
dead because of sin. The story goes on to tell that certain religious
officials walked by and ignored the man in his wounded state. The
Samaritan, a half breed (part Jew, part Gentile), stopped to minster
by pouring oil and wine on the man's wounds (the sign of the Holy
Spirit and the blood of Jesus). The Samaritan put him on his own
beast and took him to a place that would take care of him. Then he
paid the price for the man's keep, saying:

*And on the morrow when he departed, he took
out two pence, and gave them to the host, and
said unto him, Take care of him; and whatso-
ever thou spendest more, when I come again, I
will repay thee.* (Luke 10:35)

On the surface, this might not have any prophetic meaning until you start looking deeper to see truth. First of all, Jesus is a hybrid, just as the Samaritans, being both God and man. Second of all, olive oil was used as fuel for the light to represent God's *light* in the temple. We know that we are the temple of God. Thirdly, wine represents Jesus's blood, which is what healed our soul by making atonement to God. Lastly, the payment was two pence, which, in Jesus's time, was equivalent to two days wages. Matthew 20:2 (YLT) says, *"And having agreed with the workmen for a denary a day, he sent them into his vineyard."* This shows that the intent of the neighbor (Jesus) was to be gone for two days before his return (second witness in the New Testament).

Yes, there are more two-day themes. I would like to share one before we move on to some more interesting evidence, which is the story of Lazarus in John 11. When Lazarus became sick, word came to Jesus. However, Jesus made an unusual choice before he responded to the message.

> *When he had heard therefore that he was sick, he abode* **two** days *still in the same place where he was. Then when Jesus came, he found that he had lain in the grave* **four** days *already* (John 11:6–17)

Now as you read the story, you will see all kinds of neat stuff like Jesus making reference that he is the resurrection. In addition, Mary acknowledges that she knows Lazarus would rise again on the *last day*. This passage is just full of things we have already discussed. However, this time, I want to point out the time periods. Lazarus is a Jew. In this story, he is representing the Jewish people or, in a broader term, the descendants of Abraham. Jesus stayed away from him for two days after knowing he was sick. In like manner as Hosea, God stayed away from the Jews for two days before coming to raise them up. Now when he came to raise Lazarus, the passage indicated in verse 17 that Lazarus had been dead for four days. Now if we place ourselves at the time of the future resurrection and look backwards we will realize that at that time, within four thousand years (four divine days), Abraham received the covenant and the promises of God. This period would allow for *two days of sowing* and *two days of reaping*.

There is another story about this two-day or two-thousand-year time period. To understand it, you have to go back to the king of Egypt's dream about the seven-year famine. In the pharaoh's first dream, there were seven cows that came out of the river. The seven cows represented seven years. Keep this is mind as you read this as it becomes very important.

In the gospels, there is an account of a man that had an unclean spirit. Jesus freed the man. In this account, there is a revelation as to the time when uncleans spirits will be removed from their hold on humanity. This is prophesied in the book of Zechariah, *"And it shall come to pass in that day, saith the Lord of hosts, that I will cut off the names of the idols out of the land, and they shall no more be remembered: and also I will cause the prophets and the* unclean spirit to pass out of the land"* (Zech. 13:2).

The sign or revelation of when this takes place is found in Mark chapter 5. This account is also located in Matthew 8. I will use Mark's account and then add a verse from Matthew for additional information.

> *And they came over unto the other side of the sea, into the country of the Gadarenes. And when he was come out of the ship, immediately there met him out of the tombs a man with an unclean spirit, who had his dwelling among the tombs; and no man could bind him, no, not with chains: because that he had been often bound with fetters and chains, and the chains had been plucked asunder by him, and the fetters broken in pieces: neither could any man tame him. And always, night and day, he was in the mountains, and in the tombs, crying, and cutting himself with stones. But when he saw Jesus afar off, he ran and worshipped him, And cried with a loud*

*voice, and said, What have I to do with thee, Jesus,
thou Son of the most high God? I adjure thee by
God, that thou torment me not.* (Mark 5:1–7)

Matthew adds:

**And, behold, they cried out, saying, What have
we to do with thee, Jesus, thou Son of God? art
thou come hither to torment us** before the time?
(Matt. 8:29)

*For he said unto him, Come out of the man, thou
unclean spirit. And he asked him, What is thy name?
And he answered, saying, My name is Legion: for we
are many. And he besought him much that he would
not send them away out of the country. Now there
was there nigh unto the mountains a great herd of
swine feeding. And all the devils besought him, saying, Send us into the swine, that we may enter into
them. And forthwith Jesus gave them leave. And the
unclean spirits went out, and entered into the swine:
and the herd ran violently down a steep place into
the sea, (they were about two thousand;) and were
choked in the sea.* (Mark 5:8–13)

Keep in mind that Zechariah's prophecy and the pharaoh's
dreams are relevant. First, Mark said they were in the country of the
Gadarenes. In the Greek language, this means "reward at the end."
This sets the tone for the event that is unfolding.

This story is showing the reward of the unclean at the end.
Jesus, in his mercy and grace, cast out these unclean spirits out of
the man. When the spirits came Jesus asked them for their name,
they said, "Are you going to torment us before the time?" The spirits
knew they are going to lose. This story also reveals the time of their
judgment. They then told Jesus that their name was legion. This is
a military term because at the time of Jesus's return, there is going

to be a war (Armageddon). The spirits then asked permission to go into a swine. Keep in mind that swine is a physical form of uncleanness and the spirits are a form of spiritual uncleanness. The Holy Spirit is revealing that when Jesus returns, both physical and spiritual uncleanness will be dealt with.

These truths are shown in the scriptures. Here are two for you to chew on:

- The physical. *"Behold, the day of the Lord cometh, cruel both with wrath and fierce anger, to lay the land desolate: and he shall destroy the sinners thereof out of it"* (Isa. 13:9).
- The spiritual. *"And it shall come to pass in that day, saith the Lord of hosts, that I will cut off the names of the idols out of the land, and they shall no more be remembered: and also I will cause the prophets and* the unclean spirit to pass out of the land*"* (Zech. 13:2).

The unclean spirits ran down a steep place and drowned in the sea. The sea is a sign of death. This is reflected in the story of Pharaoh drowning in the Red Sea. In addition, this is further supported by Paul's comments that Israel was baptized in the sea. Baptism shows one's death by submersion, and rising out to water reveals the resurrection, *"And were all baptized unto Moses in the cloud and in the sea"* (1 Cor. 10:2).

One of the key revelations this passage brings to light is the number of swine that drown that day. Mark is careful through the Holy Spirit to estimate them, *"And forthwith Jesus gave them leave. And the unclean spirits went out, and entered into the swine: and the herd ran violently down a steep place into the sea, (they were about two thousand;) and were choked in the sea"* (Mark 5:13).

This does not sound too significant until you think back to Joseph's interpretation of Pharaoh's dream. Genesis 41:26–27 reads, *"The seven good kine are seven years; and the seven good ears are seven years: the dream is one. And the seven thin and ill favoured kine that came up after them are seven years; and the seven empty ears blasted with the east wind shall be seven years of famine."*

God does not change how he presents his truth. In the pharaoh's dream, each cow represented a year. A cow is a clean animal because it has a split hoof and chews the cud. A swine is an unclean animal because it has a split hoof but does not chew the cud. There are about two thousand swine noted in this story, revealing that in about two thousand years (two divine days) the unclean will be taken out of the land. This is yet another sign of the two-day period. Some of the days will be shortened, *"And except those days should be shortened, there should no flesh be saved: but for the elect's sake those days shall be shortened"* (Matt. 24:22).

I want to share yet another two-day witness in the book of John when he called Jesus the Lamb of God. I will be short because the evidence is already overwhelming. *"The next day John seeth Jesus coming unto him, and saith,* Behold the Lamb of God, which taketh away the sin of the world"* (John 1:29). Until Jesus gathers his disciples, two days will pass. Is this a coincidence? Is there anything in God's word that is random? These truths are within the stories and activities of Jesus.

After he gathered his disciples, they went to a wedding on the third day. John 2:1–2 says, *"And the third day there was a marriage in Cana of Galilee; and the mother of Jesus was there: And both Jesus was called, and his disciples, to the marriage."* Just like it was said in Hosea chapter 6, after two days, Jesus will raise us up. In the third day, the Day of the Lord, there will be a resurrection of his bride for the wedding.

So now I started praying for my second witness to the AD 2032 time frame. God always has at least two to three witnesses with any revelation. *"But if he will not hear thee, then take with thee one or two more,* that in the mouth of two or three witnesses every word may be established"* (Matt. 18:16). This is why Joseph had two dreams and why Pharaoh had two dreams. Each dream bore witness to the other—or, as Joseph said, "They are one."

The second witness started with the fig tree. First, let's look at the passage containing the story. Please understand that God uses different trees and plants to illustrate Israel in his stories and parables.

For the Lord thy God bringeth thee into a good land, a land of brooks of water, of fountains and depths that spring out of valleys and hills. A land of wheat, and barley, and vines, and fig trees, and pomegranates; a land of oil olive, and honey. (Deut. 8:7–8)

The list of the trees, vines and plants that illustrate Israel's blessing in the land speak to the identity of Israel. God uses the bread of life because of wheat, barley, and the manna that fell in the wilderness. The fruit of the vine in many Old and New Testament stories points to grapes and wine. Fig trees point to Israel in stories and parables as the nation itself. Pomegranates were in the tabernacle. The olive trees speak of the anointing and fuel (oil) for the temple lights. It's a land flowing with milk and honey.

So now we know why God uses these particular illustrations to show what is going to happen to Israel. *"And when he saw a fig tree in the way, he came to it, and found nothing thereon, but leaves only, and said unto it, Let no fruit grow on thee henceforward forever. And presently the fig tree withered away"* (Matt. 21:19). Jesus came upon a fig tree that did not bear any fruit. This event illustrates what Hosea had already told them. Once they had sowed the seed, their labor was finished, and the Gentiles are going to take over for their two days of reaping. Echoed in Jesus's statement, "Let no fruit grow on thee henceforward forever," Israel will not have any fruit in the harvesting of souls. Their job was to produce the seed. That they did by the grace of God through the covenant with Abraham. The works of the law do not complete the harvesting of fruit. It is by the preaching of faith that allows God's grace to empower the believer, *"For by grace are ye saved through faith; and that not of yourselves: it is the gift of God"* (Eph. 2:8).

Now let's look at the parable of the fig tree, which has the second witness contained in it:

Now learn a parable of the fig tree; When his branch is yet tender, and putteth forth leaves, ye know that summer is nigh. (Matt. 24:32)

Summer is the time where light is the strongest. We know that the fig tree is Israel because it is one of the blessings of the land. When his branch is yet tender and "putteth forth leaves," it describes the time when Israel came back into the land and became a nation in 1947. This is no doubt the time that Isaiah spoke of when he said, *"Who hath heard such a thing? who hath seen such things? Shall the earth be made to bring forth in one day? or shall a nation be born at once? for as soon as Zion travailed, she brought forth her children"* (Isa. 66:8). Zion travailing is the tribulation when the nation's eyes will be opened. After that, she brought forth her children, all the natural and adopted children in the covenant of Abraham through Jesus. This is the resurrection of the dead on the Day of the Lord, the children of light.

> *And said, By myself have I sworn, saith the Lord, for because thou hast done this thing, and hast not withheld thy son, thine only son. That in blessing I will bless thee, and in multiplying I will multiply thy seed as the stars of the heaven, and as the sand which is upon the sea shore; and thy seed shall possess the gate of his enemies.* (Gen. 22:16–17)

> *So likewise ye, when ye shall see all these things, know that it is near, even at the doors. Verily I say unto you, This generation shall not pass, till all these things be fulfilled.* (Matt. 24:33–34)

These things being fulfilled are a reference to all the events of the Olivet Discourse, which is found in Matthew chapter 24. But what I want to focus on is the phrase, "This generation shall not pass till all things be fulfilled." First, we must understand what a generation is. There is a lot of speculation as to the time of generations, however, it is not that hard to find out what Jesus meant.

So all the generations from Abraham to David are fourteen generations; and from David until

the carrying away into Babylon are fourteen generations; and from the carrying away into Babylon unto Christ are fourteen generations. (Matt. 1:17)

If you go back and count how many people are from Abraham to David in the first chapter of Matthew, you will find out there are fourteen people. Do the same from David to Babylon and Babylon to Christ, and you will find out the same thing again. Therefore, a generation is the life span of a person. So then the question becomes, how long is a person's life span? Is it found in the Bible? Yes, it is.

The days of our years are threescore years and ten; and if by reason of strength they be fourscore years, yet is their strength labour and sorrow; for it is soon cut off, and we fly away. (Ps. 90:10)

This psalm is defining the life span or length of a generation. A few things need paying attention to in this passage. A score is equal to twenty years, so threescore and ten would be seventy years and fourscore would be eighty years. An important point to understand is that seventy-nine is still in the seventieth decade. What I mean is threescore ten and nine more (seventy-nine) is not fourscore (eighty). Also, fourscore and nine (eighty-nine) is not fourscore and ten. The life span under this passage could be from seventy to eighty-nine years and still stay with the flow of time, the passage points out.

The second thing I want to point out is, *if by strength* they be in the fourscore range, spoken of in this passage is a key to the timing we will discuss later. So my conclusion is that from 1947, you could add up to eighty-nine years to stay within the generation. I started to pray about what this might mean. A long time passed before the answer came. I was elated when I understood what God was showing me.

In order to understand this second witness to the AD 2032, the Lord took me back to the first time Israel came into the land.

Remember we discussed earlier that the Gentiles were grafted into the olive tree via Christ. Now consider the exodus of Israel out of Egypt as a foreshadowing of the time we will come into the land in the Day of the Lord. Israel was held as slaves in the world. God, not wanting his wife (the nation of Israel), to be taken and held by the pharaoh any longer, the same way Abraham's wife Sarah was taken and held (Gen. 12:15), God sent Moses to lead Israel out of bondage. So consider that of all the people who came out of Egypt, only two came into the promised land, Joshua and Caleb. After Israel wandered in the wilderness for forty years, Joshua, Caleb, and the remnant of Israel got to cross over Jordan and enter the promised land. In the foreshadowing of this event, it is evident that Moses could not go in because he was representing the law and he became disqualified by transgression.

Now Joshua, which is Hebrew for Jesus, is the ruler who must lead the chosen people into the promise land. So what is Caleb a sign of? The answer to that question is in the name. Caleb, in Hebrew, means "dog." *Dog* was a term used to describe the Gentiles. For example, according to Psalm 22:16, *"For* dogs *have compassed me: the assembly of the wicked have enclosed me: they pierced my hands and my feet."* This passage is speaking of the Roman soldiers, as Gentiles, who crucified the Lord. In the New Testament, we read Jesus's word when speaking to a gentile woman, *"It is not meet to take the children's bread, and cast it to* dogs*"* (Matt. 15:26).

Therefore, not only did Caleb have the dog name, he was also a Gentile. Yet he, like us (who are Gentiles) received his inheritance through adoption into the tribe of Judah. God said that he had another spirit with him (Num. 14:24). So do we, the Holy Spirit. Caleb was a sign to all who read this account that the Gentiles were going to be adopted and receive their lot in the promised land. So why is he so important? It was his life span or age at the time of receiving his inheritance along with the rest of Israel. Let's listen to Caleb's own account of how he entered the promise land:

> **Forty years old was I when Moses the servant**
> **of the Lord sent me from Kadeshbarnea to espy**

out the land; and I brought him word again as it was in mine heart. Nevertheless my brethren that went up with me made the heart of the people melt: but I wholly followed the Lord my God. And Moses sware on that day, saying, Surely the land whereon thy feet have trodden shall be thine inheritance, and thy children's forever, because thou hast wholly followed the Lord my God. And now, behold, the Lord hath kept me alive, as he said, these forty and five years, even since the Lord spake this word unto Moses, while the children of Israel wandered in the wilderness: and now, lo, I am this day four-score and five years old. As yet **I am as strong this day as I was in the day that Moses sent me:** *as* **my strength** *was then,* **even so is my strength now,** *for war, both to go out, and to come in.* (Josh. 14:7–11)

Caleb was eighty-five years old when he received his inheritance in the promise land, the same land that Jesus will bring Jews and Gentiles into upon his return. Caleb, who represents the Gentiles, said it was by the strength that God gave him that he was able to lay claim of his inheritance. That is the strength of grace. This is the same verbiage used in Psalms to describe a person in their fourscore years, "if by reason of strength," that life span would be achieved.

The days of our years are threescore years and ten; and **if by reason of strength** *they be four-score years, yet is their strength labour and sorrow; for it is soon cut off, and* **we fly away.** (Ps. 90:10)

Caleb, who represents the fullness of the Gentile nations, received his inheritance at eighty-five years from the point of being born into the kingdom. "We fly away" pertains to the resurrection.

We shall fly away to meet the Lord in the air. So Israel was reborn in AD 1947 (the time when the parable of the fig tree came to pass) and Hosea is pointing to AD 2032. The time between 1947 and 2032 is eighty-five years, the life span of Caleb when he received his inheritance in the promised land. I think that makes a pretty good second witness to time of the Day of the Lord, with one exception:

> *And except those days* **should be shortened, there should no flesh be saved: but for the elect's sake those days shall be** **shortened**. (Matt. 24:22)

So how long is he going to shorten the days? I have no revelation on this. That is why I believe he said no one knows the day or the hour. This does bring in an interesting thought, if he had not showed us an appointed time in his word, why would he have to say that he was going to shorten them? So why would he say to learn the parable of the fig tree if we could not learn it?

The best way to conceptualize this revelation is to look at it like this—Jesus, as a man, was crucified and laid in the midst of the earth (darkness and death). On the third day (after two earth days had passed), he came back to life as the first fruits of the resurrection. This resurrection made God and man one body, heaven and earth as one. Jesus, as the Son of God, sits in the midst of heaven (light and life), will arise on the third day (after two divine days or two thousand years), and on the third day (the Day of the Lord) will make heaven and earth one.

Let's sum up this chapter. Jesus is going to return, it appears to be near or before AD 2032. I am not saying I know that it is 2032. I am just showing what my years of study are leading me to. So when the day and hour does come, are you ready?

Is the Daylight for Everyone?

> *Woe unto you that desire the day of the Lord!* to
> what end is it for you? *the day of the Lord is dark-*
> *ness, and not light. As if a man did flee from a lion,*
> *and a bear met him; or went into the house, and*
> *leaned his hand on the wall, and a serpent bit him*
> *Shall not the day of the Lord be darkness, and not*
> *light? even very dark, and no brightness in it?*
> —Amos 5:18–20

For unbelievers, the Day of the Lord will not be a time of celebration. For those who are unprepared because they love this world, this
day will be the start to their worst nightmare. One of the pictures
God paints for us is during the first part of the exodus from Egypt.
Egypt is a metaphor for the world's system. When God delivered
Israel from their slavery, the pharaoh wanted them back so he took
his army and pursued Israel to the Red Sea. God made a distinction
between those in covenant with him as those who weren't by placing
a representation of his day.

> *And the angel of God, which went before the camp*
> *of Israel, removed and went behind them; and the*

*pillar of the cloud went from before their face, and
stood behind them: And it came between the camp
of the Egyptians and the camp of Israel; and it was
a cloud and darkness to them, but it gave light
by night to these: so that the one came not near the
other all the night.* (Exod. 14:19–20)

*And it came to pass, that in the morning watch the
Lord looked unto the host of the Egyptians through
the pillar of fire and of the cloud, and troubled the
host of the Egyptians.* (Exod. 14:24)

For the unbelievers, the Day of the Lord will be a morning of
darkness, ending with an everlasting fire.

Also in the book of Malachi chapter 3 is the same theme and
warning that you must be ready for the day of his coming. Verse one
reveals Jesus's first coming, which is what prepares us for his second
coming (the Day of the Lord) in verse two:

*Behold, I will send my messenger, and he shall pre-
pare the way before me: and the Lord, whom ye seek,
shall suddenly come to his temple, even the messenger of the covenant, whom ye delight in: behold, he
shall come, saith the Lord of hosts.* But who may
abide the day of his coming? *and who shall stand
when he appeareth? for he is like a refiner's fire, and
like fullers' soap.* (Mal. 3:1–2)

Now we know why Jesus comes in the clouds with his light
shining. To the ones who are not prepared, as the virgins who let
their lamps go out, this will be a dark day. This explains why Malachi
is giving a warning to those who long for this day and are not ready
for it. Jesus is coming, and he will be glorious. You better be ready for
his light it is a very weighty thing.

*Wherefore we receiving a kingdom which cannot be
moved, let us have grace, whereby we may serve God
acceptably with reverence and godly fear: For our*
God is a consuming fire. (Heb. 12:28–29)

God is the most joyous, kind, and loving being to ever exist. He
is goodness. His grace reaches farther than anyone can imagine, but
we must receive this grace.

*That was the true Light, which lighteth every man
that cometh into the world. He was in the world,
and the world was made by him, and the world
knew him not He came unto his own, and his own*
received him not. (John 1:9–10)

God did not sacrifice his Son in vain. He died so we would be
cleansed from our sin and live a life that is holy, faithful, and grace-
filled. He knows who has received him, who has not, and who is
playing games. Everyone who received his light *is changed*, forsaking
their sins. For those who do not have the wisdom to forsake their
sins, the power of grace has not been received. Grace is not simply
forgiveness, but the power to overcome. If received, you will be more
than conquerors (Rom. 8:37). In these last days, the commitment
of so many has been diluted, watered down by men's opinions until
they are no longer profitable to the Lord.

*I am the true vine, and my Father is the husband-
man Every branch in me that beareth not fruit he
taketh away: and every branch that beareth fruit,
he purgeth it, that it may bring forth more fruit.*
(John 15:1–2)

It is important that we abide in his light by keeping his commandments, which are completed by love. If we are not abiding in
his love, we will not be able to stand in his light. I am not talking
about works; I am talking about surrendering. Simply saying "I

acknowledge my sin (weakness). Forgive me, I can't overcome on my own," I receive your gift, and I am in agreement with you. It has set me free every time. All sin is a disagreement with God. Two cannot walk together if they do not agree, *"Can two walk together, except they be agreed?"* (Amos 3:3). I am not talking about keeping all 613 commandments of the law, I am talking about keeping Christ's commandments. *"And this is his commandment, That we should believe on the name of his Son Jesus Christ, and love one another, as he gave us commandment"* (1 John 3:23).

If you will not receive this, then take heed to this verse if you are still alive at that time:

> *Enter into the rock, and hide thee in the dust, for fear of the Lord, and for the glory of his majesty. The lofty looks of man shall be humbled, and the haughtiness of men shall be bowed down, and the Lord alone shall be exalted in that day. For the day of the Lord of hosts shall be upon every one that is proud and lofty, and upon every one that is lifted up; and he shall be brought low.* (Isa. 2:10–12

Those who are not ready will stay out of his light. Those who retreat from his light will suffer the plague.

> *And this shall be the plague wherewith the Lord will smite all the people that have fought against Jerusalem; Their flesh shall* **consume away** *while they stand upon their feet, and their eyes shall consume away in their holes, and their tongue shall consume away in their mouth.* (Zech. 14:12)

The Day of the Lord will shine. For the nations that don't fear God and have attacked his people (Israel), the incorruptible light will shine on the corruptible people. When incorruptibility shines on corruption, there is a consummation.

> **And it shall come to pass in that day, that a great tumult *from the Lord shall be among them; and they shall lay hold everyone on the hand of his neighbor, and his hand shall rise up against the hand of his neighbor.* (Zech. 14:13)**

The tumult this passage is referring to has happened before with Gideon in the battle with the Midianites. The story of Gideon is a foreshadowing of the Day of the Lord. Each part of this story reveals truths about the divine day. Let's look at the story of Gideon and the Midianites I will pull out the verses that are revealing the signs. You should read the story in full Judges 6 and 7. Judges 6:1 notes, *"And the children of Israel did evil in the sight of the Lord: and the Lord delivered them into the hand of Midian seven years."*

In the days of the Midianites, Israel sinned against the Lord with Idolatry. They worshiped the wrong god(s). Israel in our day is worshiping the right God in the wrong manner. Instead of acknowledging Jesus the light as the Son of God and approaching God through him, they are pursuing the rebuilding of the temple. What they think will please God and bring his presence will actually arouse his anger and allow the antichrist to come into power. The reason the antichrist is able to arise to power is because Israel returns to Temple worship and animal sacrifice. Jesus has fulfilled the law. Returning to the old way of worship opens the door for the tribulation.

The Midianites were the seed of Abraham by his second wife.

> **Then again Abraham took a wife, and her name was Keturah. 2. And she bare him Zimran, and Jokshan, and Medan, and Midian, and Ishbak, and Shuah.** (Gen. 25:1–2)

This truth is showing that the children of Israel will be troubled by another one of the seeds of Abraham. However, instead of it being the Midianites, it will be the Ishmaelites. If you remember, I mentioned that Egypt is the metaphor for the world. The union of Abraham and Hagar (an Egyptian) produced the seed that will take Midian's place in the tribulation.

> *And the hand of Midian prevailed against Israel: and because of the Midianites the children of Israel made them the dens which are in the mountains, and caves, and strong holds.* (Judg. 6:2)

The Midianites (Abraham's other seed) made Israel run to the caves of the rocks and dens in the mountains. The promised seed of Abraham will cause Abraham's flesh seed, which was rooted in the world, to do the same.

> *Enter into the rock, and hide thee in the dust, for fear of the Lord, and for the glory of his majesty.* (Isa. 2:10)

> *And the heaven departed as a scroll when it is rolled together; and every mountain and island were moved out of their places And the kings of the earth, and the great men, and the rich men, and the chief captains, and the mighty men, and every bondman, and every free man, hid themselves in the dens and in the rocks of the mountains And said to the mountains and rocks, Fall on us, and hide us from the face of him that sitteth on the throne, and from the wrath of the Lamb: For the great day of his wrath is come; and who shall be able to stand?* (Rev. 6:14–17)

Reaping and sowing, whatever you do to someone else, good or bad, you will reap a harvest.

Israel cried out to God, and he sent them a deliver Gideon. In this story, Gideon was threshing wheat in the wine press. This is pointing to the place of the sacrament because bread is made from wheat and wine is made in the wine press. This foreshadows Jesus's death. Gideon then makes a sacrifice to God because in order to get what you want, you must give the thing you want away. Gideon sacrifices a kid, flesh, and unleavened bread. This points to Jesus's sacrifice on the cross. His flesh is the unleavened bread of life. God requires another sacrifice of a bull seven years old (the time of their sin) and tearing down the altar of Baal.

> *Then all the Midianites and the Amalekites and the children of the east were gathered together, and went over, and pitched in the valley of Jezreel.* (Judg. 6:33

Amalekites were descendants of Esau, so are those of modern-day Palestine. These people match this end-time scenario. They all gathered in the valley of Jezreel, which is the same valley as Armageddon. God tells Gideon that there are too many people so they were told that whoever is fearful and afraid could leave, and twenty-two thousand left. Anyone who is fearful and afraid is not of faith. It takes faith to please God. *"But the fearful, and unbelieving, and the abominable, and murderers, and whoremongers, and sorcerers, and idolaters, and all liars, shall have their part in the lake which burneth with fire and brimstone: which is the second death"* (Rev. 21:8).

Once these people left, God said that there were still too many people. So God told Gideon to take them to the water to drink and everyone who lapped like a *dog* to set them apart. Remember that we talked earlier about how dogs were a sign of the Gentiles. This is repeated here to show us that the Gentiles (dogs) will be included with Israel during this battle after the resurrection. The fact that the dogs were drinking water shows that they will be partakers of the Holy Spirit, the living water.

> *And it came to pass the* **same night,** *that the Lord said unto him, Arise, get thee down unto the host; for I have delivered it into thine hand.* (Judg. 7:10)

This is setting up the pattern for the Day of the Lord with him coming as a thief in the night.

> *And the Midianites and the Amalekites and all the children of the east lay along in the valley like* **grasshoppers** *for multitude; and their camels were without number, as the sand by the sea side for multitude.* (Judg. 7:12)

In this passage, we have two different seeds of Abraham, Midian, Amalekites, and the children of the east. These groups fit the same scenario in Daniel chapters 7, 11, and 12. Midian is pointing to Babylon Iraq (the lion), Persia Iran (the bear), and Greece (the leopard) all led by the Antichrist. Iraq and Iran are now populated by the seed of Ishmael or the descendants of his people's religion. The children of Greece are spoken of in, *"When I have bent Judah for me, filled the bow with Ephraim, and raised up thy sons,* O Zion, against thy sons, O Greece, *and made thee as the sword of a mighty man"* (Zech. 9:13). The Amalekites, the descendants of Esau, also have the same Islamic religion. The "children of the East," I believe, alludes to China. The term *grasshopper* seems to be connected to the locusts of Revelation 9:3. All these groups of people will gather in the Jezreel Valley (Armageddon) to fight against the Lord.

> *And when Gideon was come, behold, there was a man that told a dream unto his fellow, and said, Behold, I dreamed a dream, and, lo, a cake of barley bread tumbled into the host of Midian, and came unto a tent, and smote it that it fell, and overturned it, that the tent lay along.* (Judg. 7:13).

This barley bread is pointing us to Jesus, the bread of life, which is the force behind the defeat of this army.

> *And he divided the three hundred men into three companies, and he put a trumpet in every man's hand, with empty pitchers, and lamps within the pitchers.* (Judg. 7:16)

The three hundred men lapped like dogs, representing the Jews and Gentiles. The trumpets are instruments that make a call to war, announce a king, and start a battle. The empty pitchers made from clay, which is dust and water, implies the flesh. The lamps located within the pitchers, represents the spirit (fire) dwelling in the flesh, the state we are in if we are born again.

> *And the three companies blew the trumpets, and brake the pitchers, and held the lamps in their left hands, and the trumpets in their right hands to blow withal: and* **they cried,** *The sword of the Lord, and of Gideon.* (Judg. 7:20)

The fact that they were in three companies point to the Father, Son, and Holy Ghost, which will be revealed during the Day of the Lord. The trumpets blowing announces the King of kings, Jesus. The calling for a gathering would be the resurrection of the saints, which is also reflected in the breaking of the clay (the flesh), resulting to the light (the spirit) inside to shine. These same events take place during the last trumpet of the seven trumpets in the book of Revelation. This is what Paul is referring to in 1 Corinthians 15:52 about the last trumpet. It is the last trumpet because after this, with no other king will be announced. There will never be another gathering called by trumpet (i.e., for war). There will never be another battle fought by men. The "sword of the Lord" is a reference to the word spoken during the battle of Armageddon, in which Jesus secures his kingdom and delivers his family Israel.

And the three hundred blew the trumpets, **and the Lord set every man's sword against his fellow,** *even throughout all the host: and the host fled to Bethshittah in Zererath, and to the border of Abelmeholah, unto Tabbath.* (Judg. 7:22)

Evil shall slay the wicked: and they that hate the righteous shall be desolate. (Ps. 34:21)

Chaos ensued as every man's sword are set against his fellow. In the Day of the Lord, God will allow the lost to slay each other, and he will fight against them with his sword (his word). I know this is a lot to digest, but my point is that this Old Testament battle contains the blueprint for the future battle of Armageddon during the Day of the Lord. This pattern displayed again in the battle of Jericho. The battle of Jericho is another witness to the battle of Armageddon. However, I will not take the time to point out all the similarities in this battle because I think you get the picture.

Let's sum up this chapter. In order for you to desire the Day of the Lord, you have to give yourself to Jesus. If you refuse him, you will be on the dark side of this day. On the other hand, if you have given your life to the Lord Jesus, it will be the greatest day because you will be resurrected and live and rein with Christ. All you need to get ready is to pray a simple prayer, confess your sin, and accept his completed work on the cross.

Let's sum up this book. The Day of the Lord is the light of Jesus first shown during creation. In addition, he will shine again for a thousand years during his millennial rein. After the seventieth week of Daniel's prophecy, the sun will darken. Once this happens, the solar system will shake apart and the earth will leave its orbit. The stars of heaven will melt with fervent heat. Then the Lord will return as a thief in night during complete darkness. In this second coming, Day of the Lord, darkness (Satan) will remain in the bottomless pit until that day ends. Be ready for that day!

About the Author

Shane Carter is a born-again believer who, through a near-death experience and a visitation from the Holy Spirit, was given a gift of interpretation. This book is a product of that gift at work, along with over thirty-five years of Bible study.

Shane is a husband, father, Bible teacher, auctioneer, real estate broker, certified residential appraiser, and lead guitarist for Encompass Church's praise band.

CPSIA information can be obtained
at www.ICGtesting.com
Printed in the USA
BVHW080131210721
612415BV00008B/651

9 781098 083793